Film Actresses

Volume 19

Clara Bow

Documentary study

Part 1

ISBN-13 : 978-1502963178

ISBN-10 : 1502963175

Dtp
and
graphic design

Iacob Adrian

Author statement

The actors and actresses are the the bricks .

The cast and crew are the plaster .

They stand on the foundation created by
producers and writers and directors .

All these people creates the great palace
of the art of film .

Iacob Adrian - 2013

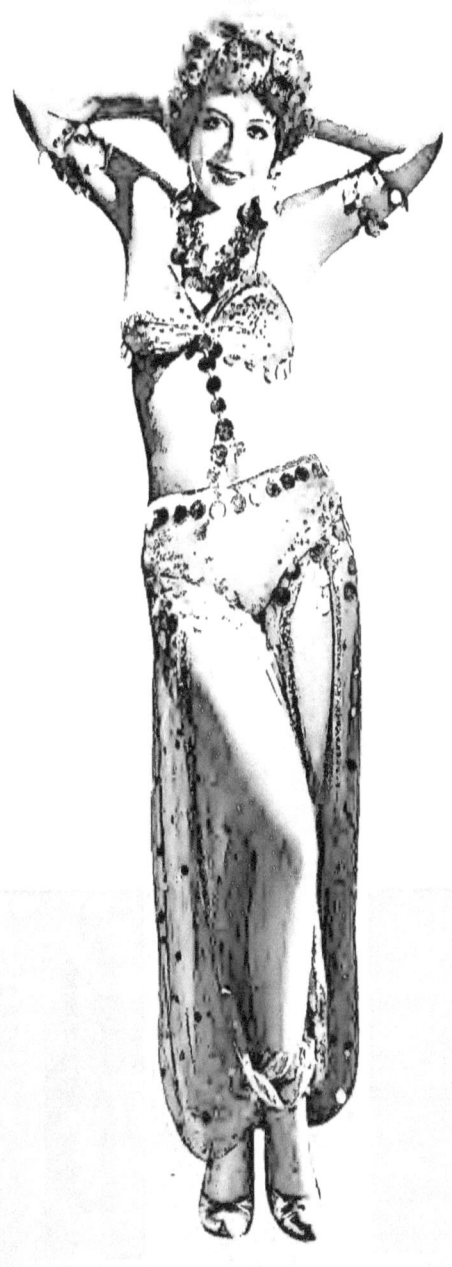

Right this way, ladies and gents,
the little lady is about to go into
her dance! *Clara Bow* becomes a
most enticing sideshow attraction
in Hoopla, her latest talkie which
is a picturization of The Barker

MOTHER CLARA

Clara Bow, Filmdom's hottest mamma, earns her real title in a way you'd least expect!

by DORA ALBERT

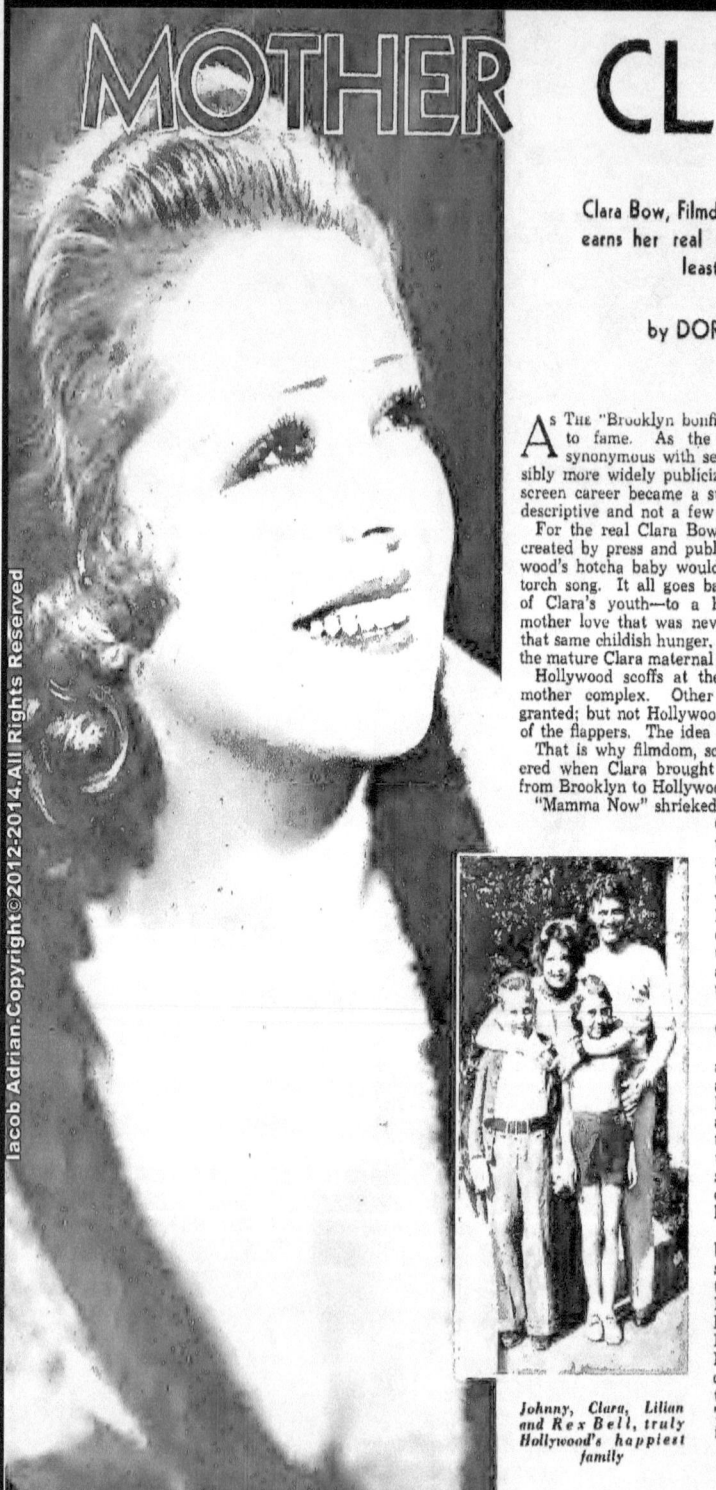

As THE "Brooklyn bonfire," Clara Bow blazed her way to fame. As the "It" girl, her name became synonymous with sex appeal the world over. Possibly more widely publicized than any other star, Clara's screen career became a succession of labels—all of them descriptive and not a few of them libelous.

For the real Clara Bow is not the madcap personality created by press and public. As a matter of fact, Hollywood's hotcha baby would rather croon a lullaby than a torch song. It all goes back to the somewhat drab days of Clara's youth—to a hungering, poignant desire for mother love that was never quite wholly satisfied. And that same childish hunger, long repressed, has developed in the mature Clara maternal instincts that will not be denied.

Hollywood scoffs at the idea of the "It" girl with a mother complex. Other stars might wax maternal—granted; but not Hollywood's hoyden and erstwhile queen of the flappers. The idea is too, too bizarre.

That is why filmdom, scenting a publicity stunt, snickered when Clara brought her twin ten-year-old cousins from Brooklyn to Hollywood to make their home with her. "Mamma Now" shrieked the headlines over a picture of Clara, and took care to enclose the word *mamma* in quotation marks. "Not to be out-done," the article read, "by other stars who have adopted a baby, Clara Bow is taking on two 10-year-old cousins. Trust Clara Bow to go the others one better. They adopt one baby and she takes on two."

● When the two children quarreled, as children will, and Lillian became homesick and wanted to go back to her home in Brooklyn, the papers again jeered at Clara. Many of the newspapers ignored the fact that Johnny said he wanted to stay forever with his famous cousin and that he wouldn't go home on a bet.

This cloud of cynicism is based entirely on misunderstanding. When Clara brought these two children with her to Hollywood, she didn't do it to keep up with the other stars. Passionate, maternal, uncalculating, she is emotionally incapable of doing anything simply to compete with anyone else. This was not even an adoption in the ordinary sense of the

Johnny, Clara, Lilian and Rex Bell, truly Hollywood's happiest family

Mother Clara

word. It might have brought greater joy and happiness into Clara's life if she had "adopted" these two cousins of hers, but she knew what hurt it would bring to her uncle and aunt. So Clara took them along to live with her, to give them clothes, schooling and the best of care, and to take from them nothing except the love that they would willingly lavish on her.

Those who have accused Clara of taking the children with her because she wanted to keep up with the rest of the Hollywood procession might like to know what really happened.

Clara has always had the urge to "mother" people. She mothered Gilbert Roland when he was young and unknown. She begged Producer Schulberg to sign him up. She mothered Gary Cooper when he was shy and unhappy. She said so herself. She admitted once, "I felt something like Gary's mother. I wanted to rumple his hair, listen to all of his troubles." And so it went through all Clara's love affairs, the maternal in her always dominant, until she met Rex Bell. And even with Rex, her love is partly the love of a woman for a man, partly the love of a mother for a little boy.

CLARA HAS always been fond of pets, and if you know anything about psychology at all, you know what that means. She has five baby dogs, a chipmunk and a white mouse she carries with her, and still it isn't enough. As she has more of everything else than other girls, so is her mother instinct more vital, more passionate. And never having had anything more vital to expend her mother love on, Clara has lavished it on her pets.

There's a touching little story back of the acquisition of Clara's mouse. One day she was walking in the desert near her ranch when a series of terrified squeaks attracted her attention. Looking to see what caused them, she saw a tiny gray mouse being attacked by two snakes. With her whip she drove off the snakes and picked up the tiny mouse in her hands. Clara decided to adopt him and took him with her to Hollywood. She fed him and took the best of care of him, but "Pinkie" died, because of the change in climate. Clara was as heartbroken as if she had lost a friend, and one of her friends, seeing how unhappy she was, gave her a little white mouse as a gift.

All that may seem far away from Clara's decision to give the children of her uncle certain advantages, but it is all part and parcel of the same starved mother instinct in her. You see, Clara originally wanted to take just Lillian, a small girl with dark hair and big brown eyes. But when Johnny thought he was going to be left behind, he cried as if his heart would break, and Clara just couldn't bear it. That was when Clara decided to take both Johnny and Lillian with her.

All her life Clara has been trying to blot out memories of her early years. Her own childhood was not particularly happy. That is why she welcomed the opportunity to give her small cousins the advantages which their parents could not afford.

CLARA'S BIRTH was not a source of joy to her father and mother. They lived in a tiny flat with two rooms. Two children had been born before Clara—both girls. One lived two hours, the other two days. The doctor told Clara's mother that she must never have any children, that Clara's birth might cause her death. She lived, however, after Clara was born, but it was a living death. Her fear, her anxiety, the terrible labor pains, affected her mind. There were times when she was fiercely tender, maternal, protective, and there were other times when she turned on Clara as though her child were a stranger.

And yet when her mother was not troubled by these moods she showed Clara the greatest tenderness and love. Clara, with her strange, unworldly intuition, understood and worshipped her mother. She cannot speak of her even now without choking up and great tears welling into her eyes. When her mother died Clara was desolated, but it was Clara's portion in life to go on living, even when she felt there was nothing to live for.

Her childhood memories in Brooklyn are bitter. Death was all around her, and the mocking faces of hunger, and violence and tragedy. When she was only five her grandfather dropped dead at her feet while he was swinging her. Frightful tragedy, of the kind you think exists only in a Greek play, touched everyone she knew and loved. There was one little boy she always played with and went to school with. One day after school when she was alone upstairs she heard a terrible noise. She rushed down to find that her little friend had gone too near a fire and was burning. She rolled him up in a carpet, did everything she could for him, but he died in her arms. And for months after his death she used to wake up in the night and dream she heard him calling, "Clara, Clara—help me."

You all know how she found fame and money and beauty in the strange alien world of the movies. She left the past behind her, or tried to leave it behind. She must not, dare not think of it. She must wipe out every memory, every unhappiness, every tragedy. How? How? How? The question beat against her brain. It mocked her. Her very success mocked her. How to forget? How to keep from thinking? It was thinking, remembering that was so terrible, that froze the very blood in you. She told an interviewer once, "I don't want to look into the future. I don't care. I distrust the future. If someone would lift the veil for me, I wouldn't let them. It is better not to look ahead and not to look back. I *will* not look back. I must not. And I dare not look ahead. I am afraid."

There must be no yesterday for Clara. There must be no tomorrow. Only today, today to be lived with laughter on your lips and hectic gayety. There must be no time for thought. You had to do things to forget. When pain gnawed at your heart, laugh. If memories crowded in on you, live more hectically, faster, faster, faster. And so Clara Bow's life kept on turning like a merry-go-round that didn't know where it was going but

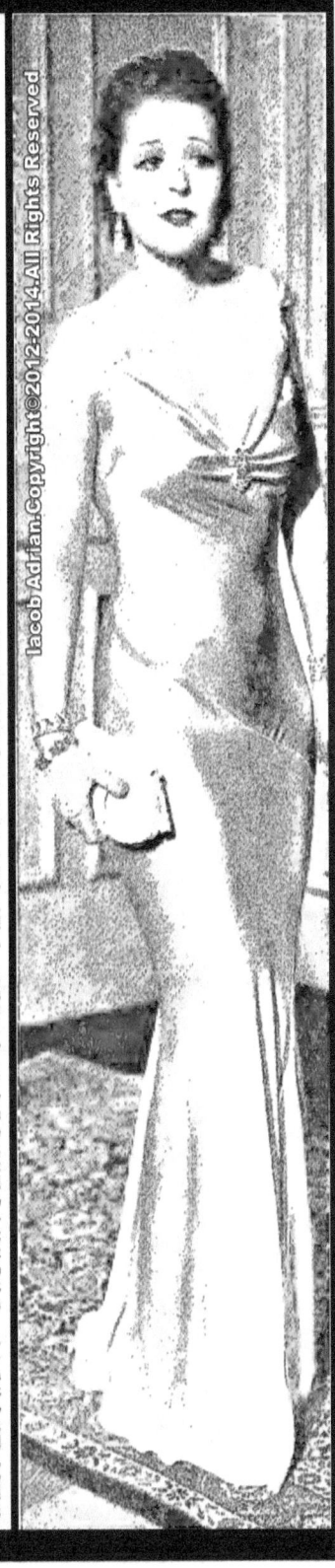

kept on and on and on . . . and underneath the hectic gayety there was a heart that was breaking.

ALL THE TIME underneath the mask she wore of a young, carefree girl, she must have been silently groping for something else. Afraid though she was of love, underneath she must have wanted to be loved by someone who would care for her, Clara, and not for her jewels or her money or her fame or publicity. She was groping for that love, groping for herself in a world of darkness. She was so terribly alone. Her friends weren't real friends. Her lovers didn't really love her. They loved themselves too much.

When Rex Bell came along, nobody in Hollywood gave him much thought. "Oh, just another boy friend in Bow's life," they said. After all, he was just a cowboy actor, and they thought that he, like all the rest of Clara's men friends, was out for what he could get from Clara. And Rex? Well, when he'd first seen Clara's pictures he hadn't liked her. It wasn't until he got to know the real Clara that he fell in love with her. Not with the screen Clara, mind you. But with that lonely little girl from Brooklyn who was trying to forget her hectic past.

Rex's mother adored Clara, still does, I guess. She felt the need of a mother in Clara's life, and she took the place of a mother to her. Rex and his mother opened up a new world to Clara. They showed her the beauties of the desert and answered the starved need of her heart for beauty. They themselves had found a measure of happiness through a certain philosophy and they gave Clara books to read about it. One of the things Clara learned, so she told me, was that if you make up your mind to do anything, there is nothing you cannot do, if you know yourself. And because she believed that, Clara, who had been afraid of the microphone and had lacked confidence in herself, was able to make her grand comeback in *Call Her Savage*. She was able to go ahead and reduce her weight to 117 when everybody but Rex and his mother told her it couldn't be done. What the new philosophy really gave Clara Bow was self-confidence.

BUT CLARA, who had gone so far from her early environment, had still farther to go before she could find herself. She wanted to get way to far horizons. New York was only one spot in the world. Ranch life, though she adored it, was only a part of life.

Europe! That was the next step. But she found when she came back to New York, after her trip to Europe, that her heart is still close to the simple things of life. She went back and visited the scenes of her childhood, and now there was no longer any need in her to forget. Peers and counts? Do they really matter? Will they ever really matter to Clara? She who had escaped as far as possible from her early environment went back to her uncle and aunt and humbly asked them to be allowed to do things for their children, her cousins.

Clara, who tried to forget, has found herself through remembering. She has found where she belongs, with her own people, her own kind, poor and humble and distraught though they may be. She has learned to think of the past without bitterness, of the future without fear.

"I'm not afraid of anything now," she told me, her eyes flashing.

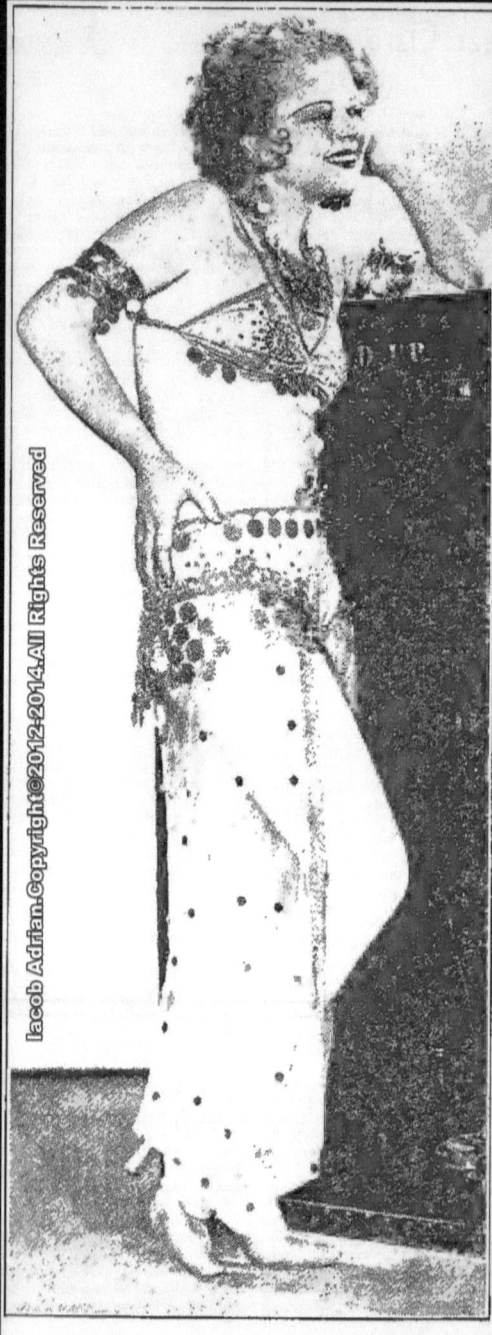

Clara Bow offers all of the appeal of the "It-girl" that endeared her to fans, in Hoopla, new talkie picturization of the stage hit, The Barker. With her appear Minna Gombell, Preston Foster, Richard Cromwell and Herbert Mundin

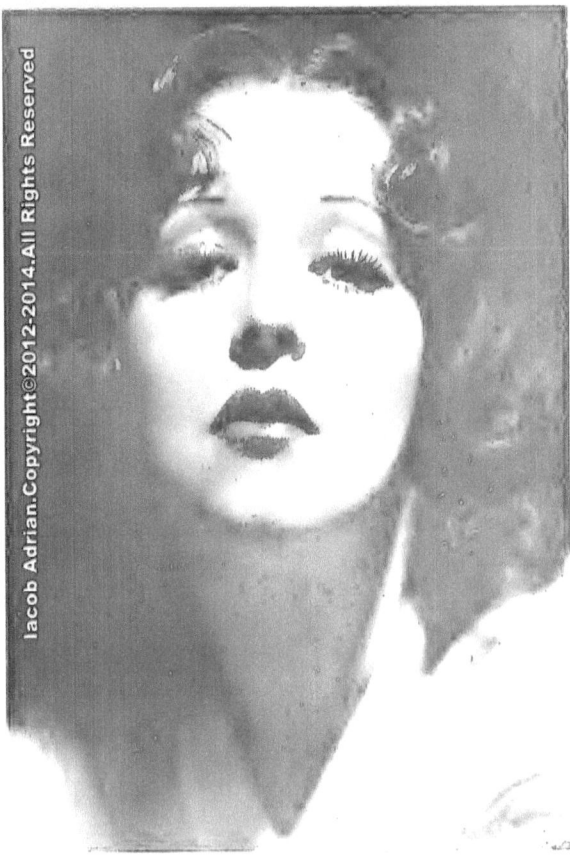

Above is the newest portrait of the "It" Girl who has been spending the last four years as Mrs. Rex Bell on a big Nevada ranch

CATCHING UP WITH CLARA BOW

What are the changes that four years retirement have made in most famous of all the flappers?

By GLADYS BABCOCK

When bewitching, red-headed Clara Bow, sparkling star of a hundred movies, "It" girl and flapper de luxe, came out of a four-year retirement a few months ago, moved back to Hollywood, and, with her husband, Rex Bell, entered into the cafe business, thousands believed she was angling for a movie "comeback."

Certainly, reasoned Hollywood wiseacres, returning to the screen was the natural thing for her to do. But that is where they were wrong.

Clara merely smiled, recalled old times and gave old friends a hand clasp that was sincere and strong, and let it go at that.

What Hollywood never dreamed of in its gay welcome, was that Clara Bow, instead of getting lonely in Rex Bell's remote Nevada ranch-house, had fallen genuinely in love with a new life—with her home, and her plans for a family. Few in Hollywood ever gave the more serious side of Clara Bow a thought. She had been the outstanding example of the frivolous mad-cap flapper. Because she looked as young and gay as ever, it was taken for granted that she still was the fun-loving girl who had danced out of Hollywood over four years ago.

"The first few months after I moved up to the ranch and Rex and I began to build our home there I was dreadfully lonely. I did miss the studios and the hustle and bustle of the sets; I missed the autograph hunters and the crowds. You can't just turn your back on a career and forget it in a moment. But I did find that being a wife and planning a home was quite the most wonderful job in the world.

"When the weeks turned into months and the duties of the ranch and of guiding the baby's first steps came, I completely forgot I had ever been a movie actress, believe it or not, until a souvenir hunter came along.

"I found that we had almost as many 'souvenir hunters' up on the ranch as they have in Hollywood. In a studio and on personal appearances visitors frequently took handkerchiefs, props from the sets or other personal and studio property for souvenirs. Up on the ranch—and 600,000 acres is a lot of front yard to watch—we found there were 'souvenir hunters' who would drive up at night in trucks and take ten or twenty cattle at a time. In the old days they used to call them cattle rustlers. Today they call them something more explosive. The rustlers with the taking ways use ten ton trucks instead of ponies. We lost more than 200 cattle in one year to these souvenir hunters.

"I've been back in Hollywood a dozen times since the first baby was born but with no thought of going back into the studios again. When the opportunity to go into business in Hollywood presented itself, Rex and I decided to divide our time between the ranch and the city but I did not move back to California with any thought of making overtures for a new movie career; I came back to be closer to Dr. H. H. Blodgett, my physician, and better nursing facilities, knowing that our second baby was no longer just a dream."

Clara's career as a wife and mother has been an expensive one. Since her retirement she has had three offers for long term contracts with major film companies ranging from $100,000 to $175,000 per picture, an offer of $150,000 plus a percentage for one picture, and two offers from independents which didn't stipulate any set figures, being profit sharing arrangements, an English film contract also was suggested.

And there were other bids—offers for radio, for endorsement of various products, for personal appearances, and for Broadway shows.

One Broadway producer offered the "It" girl $12,500 a week straight salary for a run-of-the-play contract. Another offered $11,000. Then there was an offer of $20,000 a week for a personal appearance tour of ten weeks, another at $12,500 and another for an American and European tour assuring a net salary (taxes and expenses to be paid by the sponsor) of $10,000 a week for the term of the tour. The answer was always politely but definitely "No!"

"Later—a year from now, maybe," Clara told them all, "But for some time to come I want to concentrate on being a mother." And she meant it, went back to her Hollywood hillside home, took baby Rex and his wooden horse

Catching Up With Clara Bow

and his fluffy little pooch and went out for a walk, pending Papa Rex's arrival from the ranch, for dinner.

Few film stars have ever known the fame and adoration that Clara Bow has enjoyed. There was a time when her fan mail averaged more than 37,000 letters a month. Even today—four years after the release of her second Fox picture, *Hoopla* (which she didn't like and which fans didn't care so much for either) Clara's fan mail totals several hundred letters a month and she tries to answer them all.

"Children were the one thing interviewers never discussed with me in the old days. But you could have written this story ten years ago. I felt the same way about children and marriage then. I'll always feel that way. I had to work darned hard to keep on top when I was in pictures but the hard work proved worth while. When I was ready for marriage and a family I was able to concentrate on them, and not divide my time.

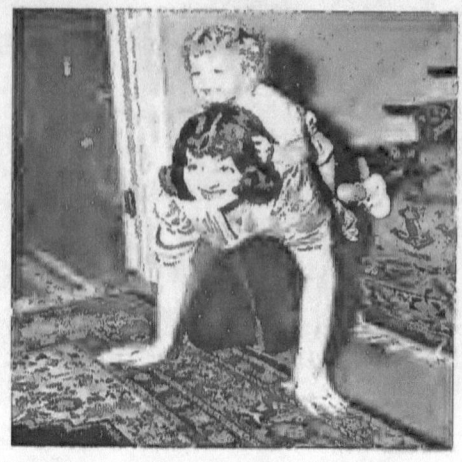

Clara Bow Bell and young Rex Larbo Bell stopped in the middle of a romp to give the cameraman two bright smiles of welcome

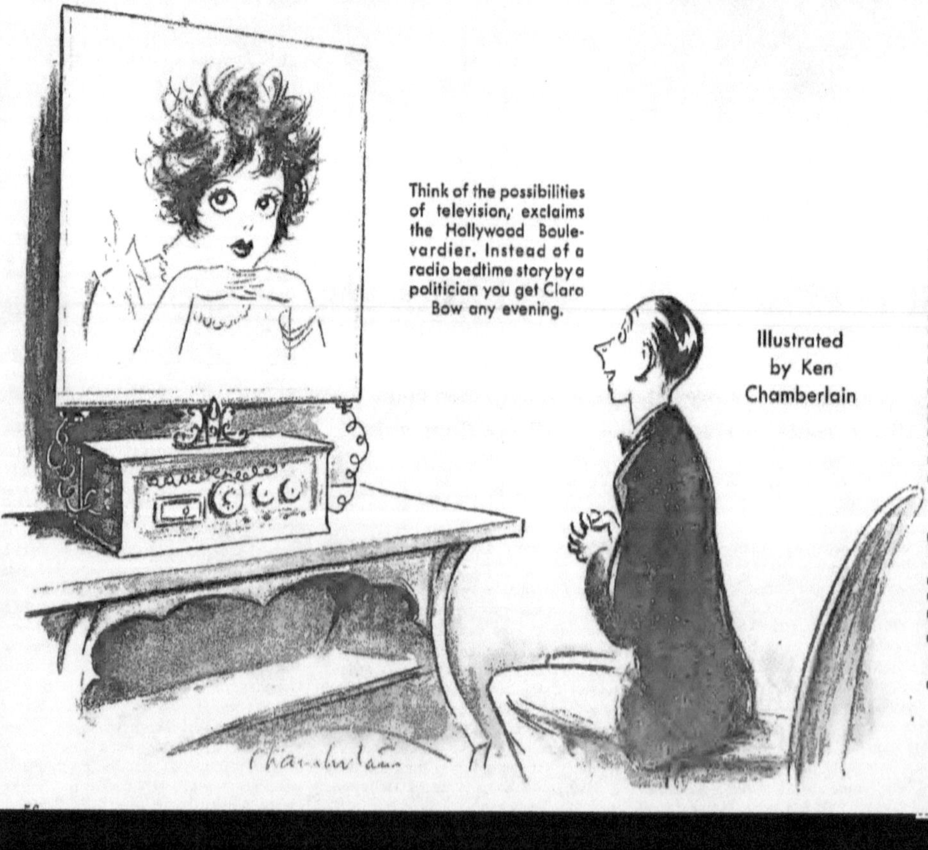

Think of the possibilities of television, exclaims the Hollywood Boulevardier. Instead of a radio bedtime story by a politician you get Clara Bow any evening.

Illustrated by Ken Chamberlain

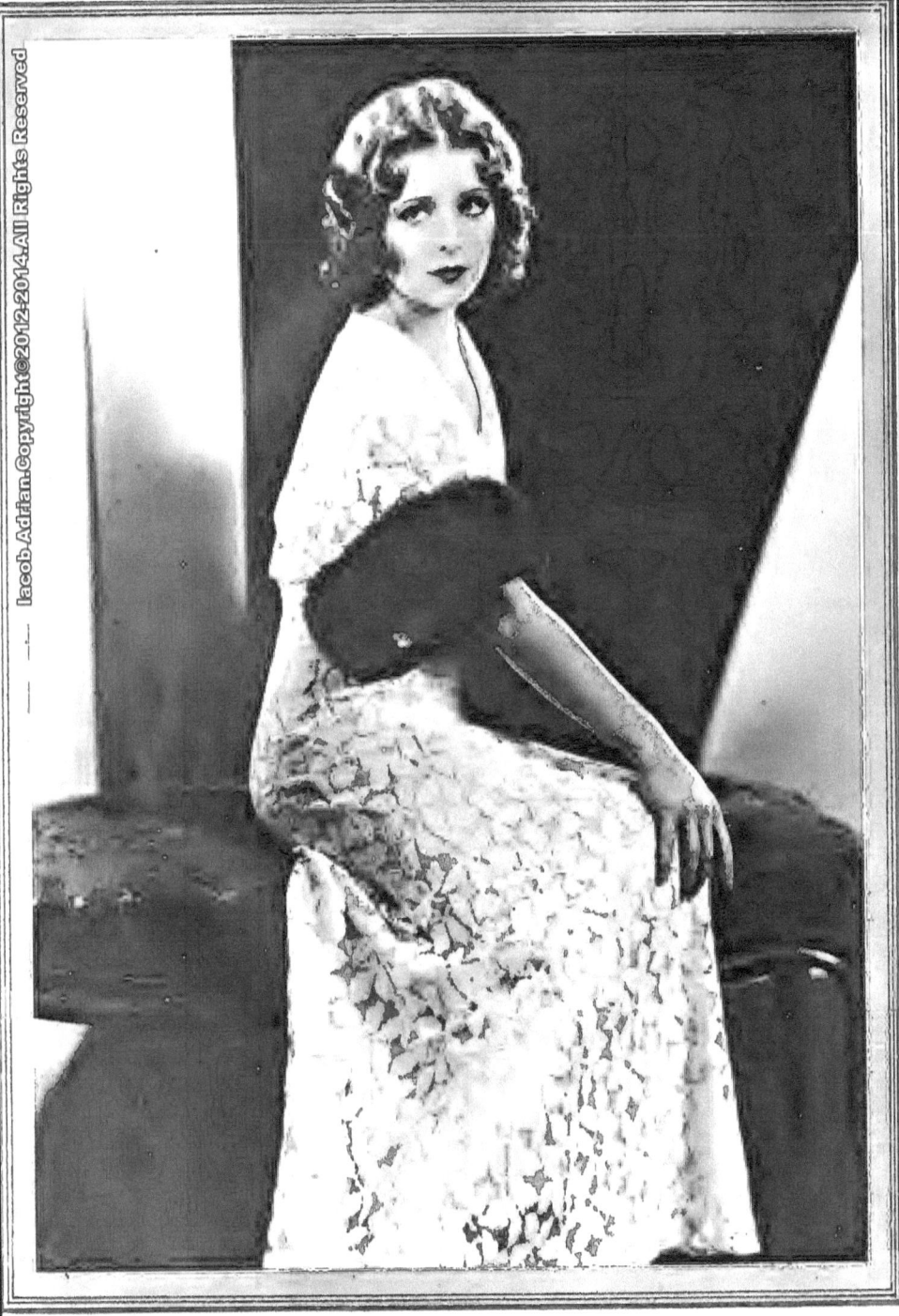

The first photo-portrait of Clara Bow made since her reducing sojourn on the
Rex Bell ranch, preparatory to her return to the films in "Call Me Savage."
She is variously reported to have taken off from twenty to thirty pounds.
After "Call Me Savage," Clara hopes to direct a picture.

JIM TULLY
ANNOUNCES

The Return of

Is the career of the "IT" girl from Brooklyn to be climaxed
with another success in her return to films in the new
Fox picture, "Call Her Savage"? Study the two pictures
of Clara to-day—and Clara as you used to know her

CLARA BOW

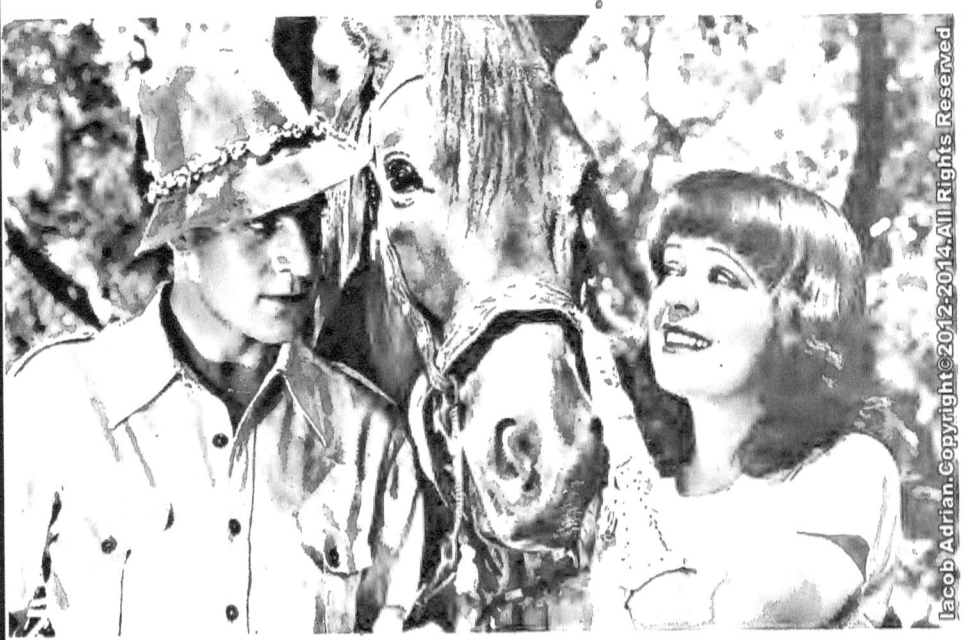

Clara Bow in one of the first scenes of "Call Her Savage," with Gilbert Roland, her leading man.

SHE has been heard to say in Hollywood, sometimes plaintively, at others belligerently, "I never want to come to town again."

Her childhood on the sidewalks of Brooklyn has left her with a dread of large cities. Her ambition is to live on a hundred thousand acres, with mountains as fences and the cloudless sky as a roof. It looks now as if she will gratify that ambition.

She has found but boredom in the adoration of millions. Gifted with something akin, at times, to great emotion on the screen, Clara Bow is a superior screen actress.

A hoyden at heart, she lacks the poise and the tremendous restraint of her brilliant little Brooklyn neighbor, Barbara Stanwyck.

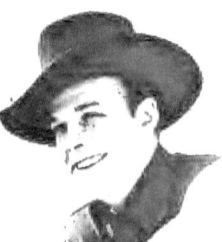

Rex Bell and his ever evident smile.

Carrying always within her the seed of high talent, which threatened, but never quite germinated into supreme greatness, she is once again back from the edge of oblivion, under the shrewd eye of Winfield Sheehan, the man who stands behind the big guns of the Fox Film Company.

That after the first Fox film, of her comeback, "Call Her Savage," she will take her place as the most popular actress in the world is the prediction of many notable critics.

In that I agree. What her faults are, I do not now remember. They are all forgotten in the fact that she is a direct and honest, if somewhat irresponsible girl.

A girl who sought love, even in headlines, there are many friends who say that she now has too much of it. For, if there is one woman in the world who will admit that a husband can be too attentive, she may possibly concede that Clara Bow's husband, Rex Bell, is that man.

But, of course, a man on a Nevada ranch, looking at the western ends of many thousands of cattle going east, cannot be blamed for being overly attentive to a damsel like Clara Bow. This error, if error it be, has been committed by men who had much more to do.

At the top of her fame, Clara Bow received far more letters than any woman on earth. Five thousand a week, they came from the far corners of the world.

English, Scotch, and French, she was born in a poor section of Brooklyn, from which she meandered, over a rocky and troubled road, to the Valley of the Screen Immortals.

Her father was a day laborer, her mother, a woman who died mad. Her childhood was turbulent and full of pain. Like many proud people, she fought sorrow with belligerence instead of calm.

Not beautiful in the strict sense, she is yet vivacious and charming. These attributes border on beauty—for Clara. She also possesses that quality, as yet unexplained by science—of "tak-

The Return of Clara Bow

ing a really good picture."

In a crowd of people who are her equals in personality, Clara Bow's photograph will stand out.

Miss Bow admits that, even as a small girl, she was never without a looking-glass. She would stand before the mirrors hours at a time and watch her varying facial expressions.

The usual procedure of parents seems to have been reversed in the exuberant Clara's case. She received complete understanding from her father, and little or none from her mother.

The years may mellow and bring more complete understanding to Clara for the distracted woman who was her mother. After all, her heart, though embittered, is as warm as her red-gold hair.

Her consideration for her father has long been one of the white lights in the self-centered city of Hollywood. He has long remained, in her own words, "the best friend I ever had."

Clara early learned to avoid her none too happy home and spent all the time possible in cheap theaters.

Residents of Brooklyn still remember a small red-headed child in the front rows of different theaters, watching intensely the gestures of now long forgotten players. Remembering what she had seen in the theater, she would return to her mirror and practice the mannerisms of the players until forced to retire.

Long before the age of puberty, she saw herself a great screen actress.

Her school books were neglected for the film magazines.

Teased by her playmates on account of her preoccupation with films, she nevertheless continued to live sturdily with her dreams.

Before long a film magazine launched a beauty contest. That the shores of Hollywood were strewn with girls who had won such contests did not daunt Clara's father.

Without telling her of his intention, the father sent a cheap photograph of Clara to the editors of the magazine. Many weeks merged into months while the hopeful father waited.

In the meantime Clara was forced to forget her ambitions and nurse her critically ill mother.

The heart of the ambitious girl smouldered in the drab home.

Each day the father went to his labor as a carpenter's helper.

One day a letter came to the house addressed to Clara Bow.

On the envelope was the address of the film magazine. "I hope it's offering her a contract," said the mail man.

The girl's father read the letter quickly to ascertain if it contained bad news, and if so, to keep it from Clara.

Instead, the letter informed Clara that her photograph had survived the semi-finals in which thousands were competing.

He told the girl the news. Overjoyed, she rushed toward her mother's room.

"Better wait," warned her father, "there's still a long ways to go."

The girl sobbed for a second.

"But you'll win," he said, "don't cry—you must never forget you're a Bow."

To this day, Clara often says of her father, "He was always a good pal to me."

Could the two at this moment have seen the road of golden fame ahead, the cheap little home might have been a palace.

The final test was two weeks off. The judges of the contest were Howard Chandler Christy, Harrison Fisher, and Neysa McMein.

The girl worried herself nearly ill during the intervening days.

On the day of the final decision, Clara dressed herself in a calico frock and went nervously forth to meet her judges.

More than a hundred girls were assembled at the offices of the magazine. Ten girls were to be selected from the gathering. Then after this torture of uncertainty, one girl was to be selected from the ten.

Little Cinderella Bow stood bravely among her better dressed competitors.

As each girl faced the judges she was handed a letter and instructed to act as if it contained bad news.

Clara waited many hours before her turn came. The emotionally sensitive girl watched many go through the motions of grief.

With long red hair falling on her shoulders, the little tomboy smoothed her wrinkled calico frock and stood before the masters of her destiny.

She took the letter carelessly, looked at it nonchalantly, while the judges and all in the room waited.

There followed an ominous silence.

The juvenile Bow's tears came slowly, as she read the letter. The paper rattled in her trembling hands.

She looked about as if death were calling.

The letter fell to the floor. A spasm of wild grief shot through the room.

Contesting girls and judges looked in astonishment at one another.

A great actress was among them.

Her competitors fell away from her like friends from the destitute.

She was promised a motion picture contract—and given an evening gown. Both signified first prize.

When her father asked her how she happened to win, she replied,

"I thought of Mother."

Happiness fluttered for a time on the door sills of the Bows.

There were only two flies in Clara's honey. She had no place to wear the gown, and there was no motion picture company who desired her services.

After a long wait she heard from a small film company. She was offered a small part, according to the terms of the magazine's contract. Her salary was five dollars a day.

She accepted.

Knowing nothing of make-up, she spent a sleepless night in quandary.

When she arrived on the director's set, that gentleman threw up his hands in despair, and exclaimed,

"Another beauty contest winner!"

She pleaded with him. He was cold as a rejection slip.

At last the great man allowed her to remain on his set—as atmosphere.

Proud at last of her chance, she rode back and forth to work—make-up and all—in the subway.

Some people snickered in the under-

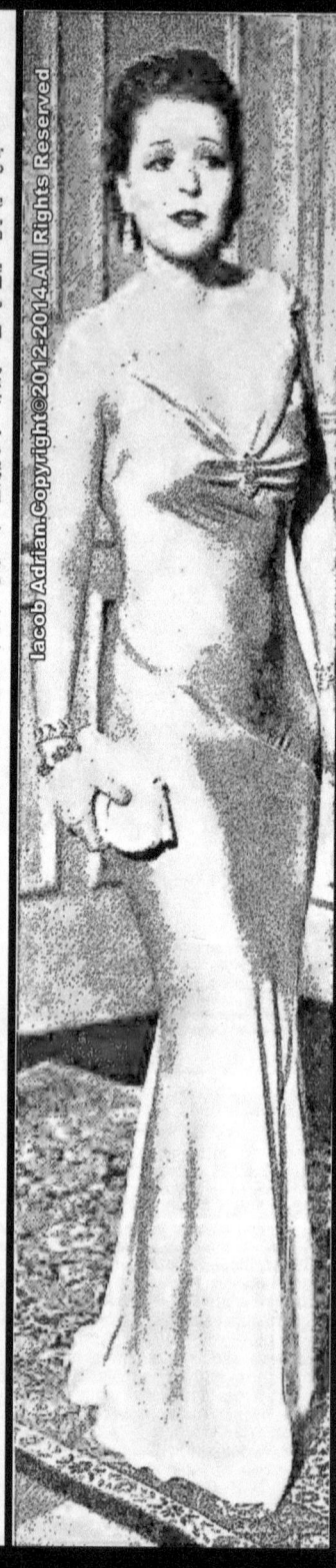

ground cars. For how were they to know that in the badly-clad body of the sad brown-eyed red-head was the soul of a mighty girl?

Her mother protested at the work she was doing. Her father approved.

Each night she rehearsed long at a time before the mirror the many phases of acting she had seen.

The picture finished, the proud Clara's father gave her sixty cents to take five of her young friends to see it.

Several reels appeared. Her friends asked when she appeared.

"Just wait," replied Clara.

They did.

All ended happily in the film.

There was sadness in the heart of the laborer's daughter.

She was not in the film.

That night she ran home and sobbed, "Daddy, Daddy, Daddy."

To see a young heart breaking is no pleasant sight for a man doomed to live in Brooklyn.

Besides, he had other troubles to bear.

He put his work-gnarled hands in her tangled red hair. Kissing her forehead, he said quietly, "I understand."

"I know you do, Daddy—and I'll be brave—for your sake."

Her father looked about the room. "You don't belong here," he said. And then, slowly, "And I don't either."

Desperate resolves were born that night.

In the early morning Clara heard her father in the kitchen preparing his breakfast. She dressed quickly and joined him.

After Clara had prepared a noon-day lunch for him, they discussed one remaining problem.

. . . Mrs. Bow could not be left in the house alone . . .

Neither would they ask neighbors to take care of their own.

It was decided that when the father's present employment had finished he would remain at home while Clara made the rounds of the studios.

He would soon have enough money to support the family two months.

For six weeks Clara appeared at many studios and found no work.

She had picked up the rudiments of stenography at school. Clara obtained a position as a typist.

Her mother's illness became more acute.

Clara failed at stenography.

Then something happened. Elmer Clifton, a director, was in search of a hoyden type of girl. As he could not afford that boon of the small producer, a "box office name," he was forced to look about for a player of talent who could be had at a cheap price.

While looking at an old magazine he came across Clara Bow's picture. Wondering if she would be able to act, he telephoned her for an appointment.

During her many trips to the studios, casting directors had always told her that she was "too young."

Dreading such a decision from Clifton, she made an effort to appear much older by arranging her long auburn hair in such a way as to add several years to her appearance.

When Clifton saw her, he gasped . . . "You look much older than your portrait. The part calls for a younger girl."

"I nearly died right there," said Clara. "It took some quick thinking and some quicker changing to convince Mr. Clifton that I could look younger. At last he agreed that I was perfect for the part '*if I could act*' . . .

The Return of Clara Bow

"He offered me forty dollars a week. I became business-like, for once, and said, 'Make it fifty'—and he did. We soon came to terms after I agreed to pay my own expenses home if I failed in the part."

The film was made at New Bedford, Massachusetts, and was called "Down to the Sea in Ships."

Still a child, Clara worked through the strenuous whaling film, alone, and returned home, exhausted.

Though it was a successful picture her name attracted but slight attention.

On her first night home, Clara awoke from a sound sleep. The light from the street made a long knife gleam above her. With startled eyes, she saw her mother's wild expression and disheveled appearance.

The knife came downward as Clara grappled with her insane mother. She was overpowered with difficulty.

Her mother died soon afterward.

With despair and loneliness, Clara walked about the streets of Brooklyn.

A conference with her father followed. As soon as financial arrangements could be made, which were not easy in their destitute circumstances, Clara departed for Hollywood, while her father remained in Brooklyn.

She missed the companionship of her father, and her money soon dwindled rapidly.

The girl with the sad brown eyes was in a short time making the rounds of the Hollywood studios.

Discouraged after weeks of unsuccessful effort, Clara wired her father for money for her ticket home.

The courageous father secured money and used it for a ticket to join his daughter in Hollywood.

Months dragged along. Father and daughter were penniless.

They had at last a flash of luck in meeting B. P. Schulberg, then an independent producer.

Schulberg saw in Clara Bow all that others had missed. He put her under contract and at the first opportunity gave her the lead in "Mantrap."

It made her famous. The rest is vivid screen history.

Madame Elinor Glyn saw her work and expressed the opinion that she had that subtle something which she defined as "It." To prove her faith, she even wrote a film play for her. It established Clara Bow.

Her later work showed conclusively that she was an actress of high ability.

In mediocre films, the personality of Clara was always transcendent.

Her triumphs ended in divorce from the screen and marriage to Rex Bell.

Fabulous offers came from all over.

At last she was persuaded to enroll under the banner of the Fox Film Company to appear in "Call Her Savage" —which should be one of the important pictures of the year.

She hopes to make six more films, and then retire to a million acre ranch, where grease paint is no more, and the only stars visible, except herself, are those that glitter in the far-off sky.

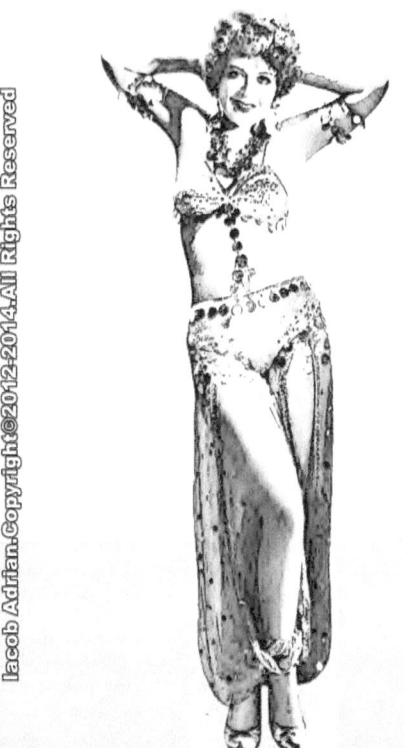

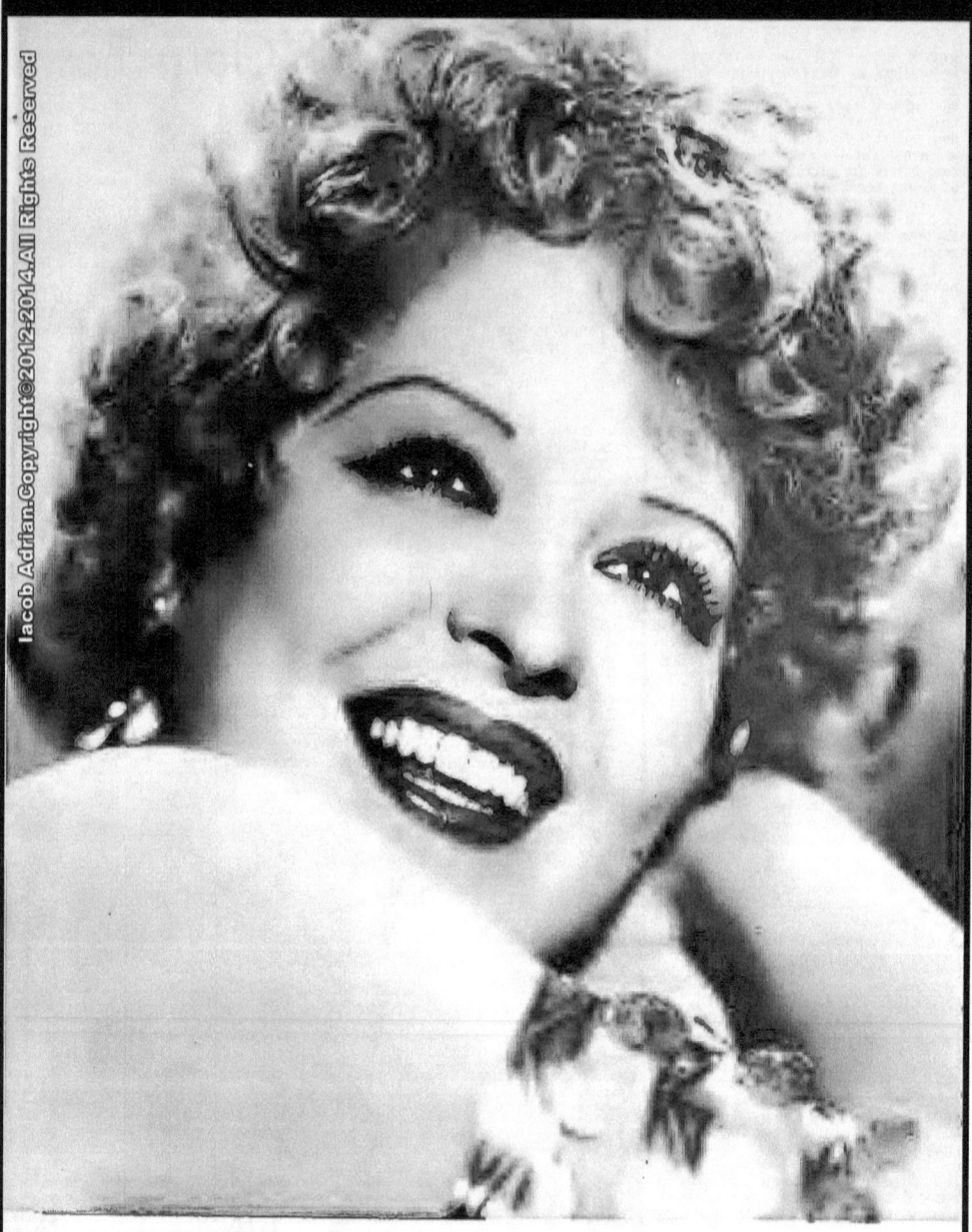

THE NEW MOVIE
MAGAZINE'S

GALLERY
OF
STARS

CLARA BOW—You will see her again in the new Fox picture, "Hoopla." Flaming-haired Clara Bow bowed into a Brooklyn cradle. A beauty contest won her her first film role in Billie Dove's "Beyond the Rainbow." Scene cut because Clara's real tears ruined her make-up. So—back to business school for a while. Rediscovered by director Elmer Clifton and featured in "Down to the Sea in Ships." Success —amid rumors and romances. Married to Rex Bell. Retired for two years. Then resumed career under Fox banner. Has no superstitions but hates being called the "It" girl. So, please don't do it.

Why CLARA BOW Can't Stay in LOVE

By RUTH WATERBURY

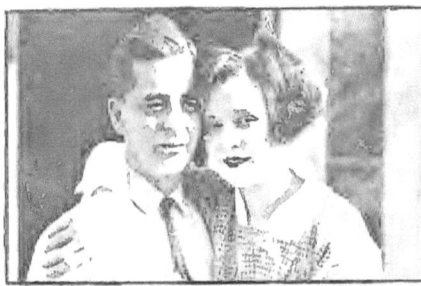

Clara Bow and her father, Robert Bow.

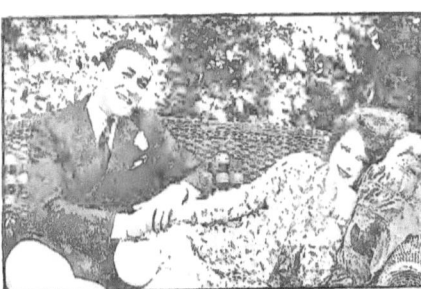

Clara and Harry Richman, the Broadway songster.

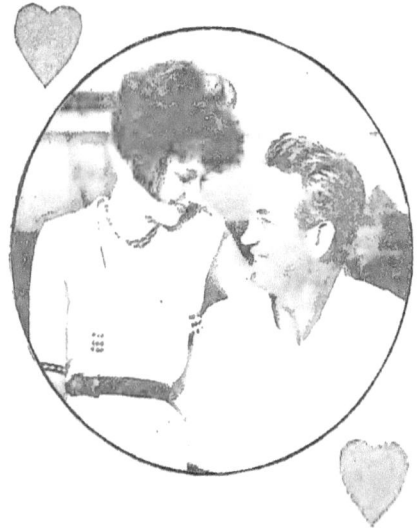

Clara with Victor Fleming, the Hollywood director.

A FEW months ago Clara Bow announced her engagement. Which wasn't exactly news. In fact, it was so little real news that the only angle of interest, as far as the press was concerned, was the man involved. The man of the engagement was Harry Richman, a curly-haired song and dance boy from Broadway, but recently arrived in Hollywood to make his first talkie.

It was summer in Hollywood and for a time the engagement looked as real as the ten-thousand-dollar diamond ring Harry had slipped on Clara's correct finger. For a time there were moonlight and roses, kisses and caresses, tête-à-têtes and love avowals, all conveniently within camera range.

It was all very wonderful, marvelous, and amorous. And it was all very swell publicity for its principals.

Then one morning, not so long ago, newspapers throughout the country carried first-page yarns to the effect that Harry and Clara weren't engaged after all; that it had all been a publicity plant in the first place; and that Clara's heart interest was somewhere else again.

Now the men in Clara Bow's engagements are never very important—not any more of importance than the men in Peggy Hopkins Joyce's marriages, for instance. Clara has been engaged to Gilbert Roland, Victor Fleming, Robert Savage, Gary Cooper, and several others. Not to mention the more recent Harry Richman.

And each time it has seemed as though, just after the announcement of the engagement, Clara's heart interest has been somewhere else again.

Clara's beaux and Cupid's bow. Why can't Clara, the "IT" girl of the screen, the girl who most perfectly typifies flaming youth and fierce desire, why can't Clara Bow stay in love?

To any one who knows her—restless, discontented, lonely as only the empty in heart are lonely—there cannot be the faintest doubt that Clara wants to be in love; that, even, she wants to marry and have children.

Many men have loved her. Obviously she could have married any number of times. Girls as gifted with beauty, youth, and fortune as Clara are very rare, indeed, and such girls are born for romance.

Yet, seemingly, Clara, who wants love so much, is afraid of it. Plainly, she runs away from romance when she discovers it near her.

A learned psychologist would remark that many people fall in love time after time, but if the psychologist were true to his teachings, he would point out that such people always fall in love with the same type.

No group could be more varied than the group Clara has fallen for. Gilbert Roland is a Mexican, darkly romantic, fiercely jealous, eager and handsome. Victor Fleming is sandy-haired, plain, but most amusing, and many years Clara's senior. Robert Savage, who burned up a lot of Hollywood Boulevard with his father's money, is just the usual rich man's son. Gary Cooper was newly come down from the hills when Clara met him, a tall, rangy, laconic youth. Harry Richman is typically Broadway, dark, suave, a wise guy, flashy and smart.

Those five men of totally different temperament are

For All Her Reported Engagements, She Hasn't Found the Right Man.

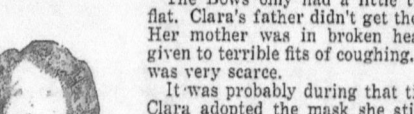

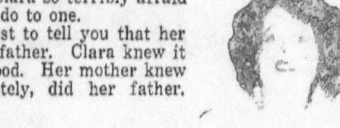

the five who could not hold Clara Bow's affections after they had once secured them.

Sometimes I wonder if it is the memory of her mother that makes Clara so terribly afraid of love and what it can do to one.

Clara would be the first to tell you that her mother never loved her father. Clara knew it from her earliest childhood. Her mother knew it. So, too, unfortunately, did her father.

The Bows only had a little two-room flat. Clara's father didn't get the breaks. Her mother was in broken health and given to terrible fits of coughing. Money was very scarce.

It was probably during that time that Clara adopted the mask she still wears today. It was probably then that she first learned you can laugh and make the

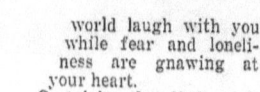

Robert Bow was the spoiled younger son of an average American family. Born and brought up close to each other in the same farming district of New York State, the girl Robert Bow married was more taught to seek the finer things of life.

They had two babies, both girls, one who lived for an hour and one who lived for a day, before Clara, who was to bring them fame, came along.

The little family moved to Brooklyn and on the pavements of that city, Clara fought her

world laugh with you while fear and loneliness are gnawing at your heart.

Certainly the little red-head went through more emotions before the age of twelve than most of us experience in an entire existence.

As a child she discovered movies and through them, beauty. And it was the movies themselves, as you know, that gave her the daring idea of entering her photograph in a contest that a screen magazine was running.

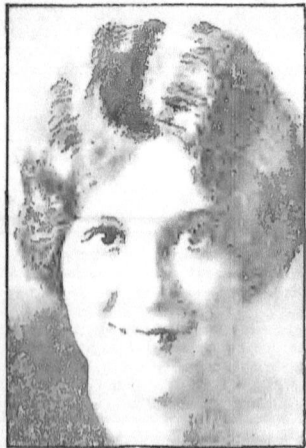

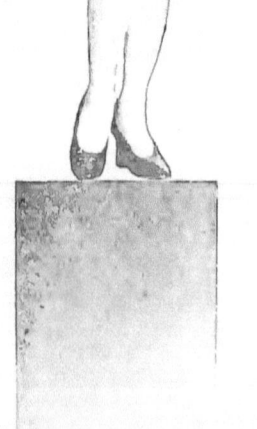

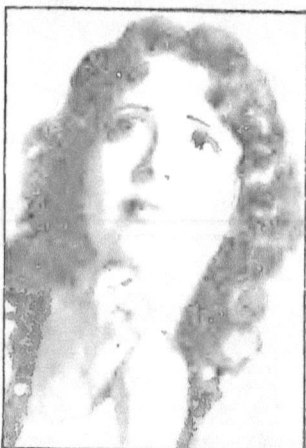

In the center is the Clara Bow the movie fans know. The IT girl of Hollywood is going to be starred next in "Station S-E-X."

way up. She was always a tomboy. Life even then had made her too hard to leave her adaptable to the silly pretentions of most girls. She went with boys and tried to be one of them. And while she tried to be the gayest of the gay, the cutest kid of the lot, her home life was as drab as anything in a Russian novel.

The pictures at the left and above shaw Clara Bow as she was when she first came to pictures, a life embittered little girl.

She won the magazine contest. The judges were famous artists, Howard Chandler Christie, Harrison Fisher, and Neysa McMein. It was probably those judges who saved her and gave her to the movie fans of today. For the artist sees deeper than the average eye and those three sane

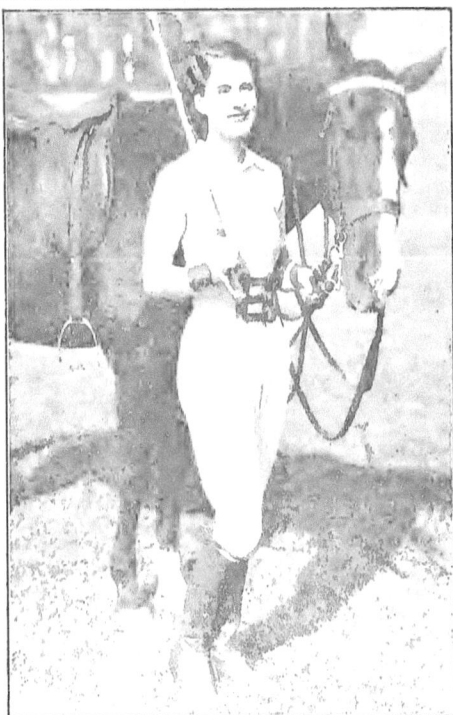

Norma Shearer, at the Midwick Country Club, near Los Angeles, where the polo scenes of her picture, "Their Own Desire," were filmed

Why Clara Bow Can't Stay in Love

people saw beyond the little Bow girl's shabby clothes into the beauty and the soul beneath them.

Here, then, entered destiny. If Clara hadn't won that contest, she would probably be married now and instead of the world's favorite flapper be a settled young matron. But the contest gave her ambition its first expression and subsequent events were to test the firmness of character her hard childhood had forced her to acquire.

Clara worked in the picture her prize-winning cast her for. She didn't know how to make-up. She lacked, completely, the right clothes. The one scene she had to play was one in which she was supposed to cry. That was easy for her. She merely thought of home.

She was through after that, except for waiting for a showing of her picture. When the film was finally released, Clara wasn't in it at all. She had bragged to all the kids in the neighborhood about her success, her future. Now she was subjected to their merciless sarcasm. Her whole little world seemed to be in ashes and it was a terrible blow to her. But a harder one was coming.

Clara haunted the movie studios. There were several of them in the East at that time. She didn't find anything. She was too young and too fat and too shabby. She soon found that being a contest winner gave her no more distinction than being feminine. There were almost as many beauty winners in the studios as there were girls. The hard part of it was that the youngster had to fight not only her own discouragement but her mother's opposition.

The strain of poverty, of loveliness, of ill health had got in at Clara's mother. She turned all her feverish frustration on Clara. She resolved the girl wasn't going to get into trouble while she had a mother to guard her. And to her morbid imagination, motion picture studios threatened her little daughter's very life. And she did her best to argue her little daughter out of her dreams.

Clara had just got her first break— the part of the little roughneck in "Down to the Sea in Ships." Fifty dollars a week, a trip to New Bedford for scenes, and a real opportunity. The girl was in the seventh heaven of delight.

Clara went away on location the next day. All the thirteen weeks, she was away, she was ill. She couldn't sleep because she would wake herself up, crying violently. Yet by day she played a nutty little kid and played it magnificently. Shortly thereafter Clara's mother died and the girl went to Hollywood. As soon as "Down to the Sea in Ships" was released, Clara's future was assured. She was too good to pass by. B. P. Schulberg, the motion picture executive, signed her for a very small company. For three years Clara worked constantly, learned constantly, tried to find herself. When Schulberg went to Paramount, he took Clara with him. It was her first chance with a big company. But more important, it gave her her first chance to take stock and for a little while to be herself.

It was about then that she fell in love—or thought she fell in love—with Gilbert Roland. I doubt very much that it was ever more than a case of youthful propinquity. They were each of them mere children of Hollywood, romantic, over-emotional, heart-hungry. Yet something might have come of it if Gilbert hadn't been so jealous, if he hadn't lost his temper and used too many words at the sight of Clara even making love for screen purposes to another man. So that blew up.

Vic Fleming was Clara's director on "Wings." I know, myself, that Clara was bewildered, lonely, unsettled during that picture. Love was all around her. Richard Arlen was courting Jobyna Ralston. The handsome young "Buddy" Rogers was around. They were out on the desert on location, under a desert moon. Clara just had to be in love with somebody, so she chose Fleming. After they returned to Hollywood, her heart returned to normal.

Robert Savage probably represented class to her. Clara is terribly conscious of her lack of education and swanky upbringing. She flapped around with young Savage, probably until she discovered, as most everybody else did, that he was more rhinestone than diamond.

Gary Cooper came along just as Clara was experiencing the heady wine of Elinor Glyn's discovering her as the IT girl; just as several of her biggest pictures smashed box-office records throughout the country. She was fussing with her hair then, getting it every color in the rainbow; fussing with her personality, making it everything from Elsie Dinsmore to Cleopatra.

Gary was shy, quiet, reserved, and amusing. He is a darling and Clara sensed it. He taught her a lot and she taught him more. But when they both got through going to school to one another, they found they didn't have so much to talk about.

Which brings us practically up to the present and Mr. Richman.

It is true that Clara did see a lot of Harry Richman the last time she was in New York. It is equally true that he is a clever boy who makes one laugh. And after a life like Clara's the wish to laugh, to be constantly amused, is the strongest urge.

Or, at least, it seems so. I believe Clara thinks that it is. I believe that is what made her agree to be engaged to Richman, even for publicity purposes. Clara wanted to laugh with Harry, play about with Harry. She was willing to give it a try.

The only trouble was that Clara has climbed higher than she knows. The disturbing factor was her intuitive understanding of emotion, that subtle, lovely understanding that makes her the actress that she is.

In her work, Clara is turning more and more from the jazz kids she has played to the great characters she is worthy of playing. She is ceasing, while still in her earliest twenties, to play girls and is demanding the right to play women.

So is her heart changing without her knowing it and her mind and her soul are demanding a man in her life—a man in the truest meaning of the word —and not a playboy an actor, or a poseur.

Whether she knows it or not, half of her love for the men in her life has been maternal. The love for young Gilbert Roland, when she was struggling and he was quite unknown; a sort of fostering love for Robert Savage; the sophisticated love she brought Gary Cooper, when he was trying to find himself.

Maternal love when it is itself— when it is truly the love between mother and child—is the most beautiful thing in the world. But the real love that a woman gives to the man to whom she gives her whole heart is not maternal at all, nor should it be.

Yet a woman can only give her whole heart to a man who commands it and who gives her something in return.

That is the kind of man Clara Bow is searching for today. She hasn't found him. Perhaps she never will, though she deserves him.

But it is the real answer to why she can not stay in love. Clara Bow has not stayed in love because to date she had never yet been there.

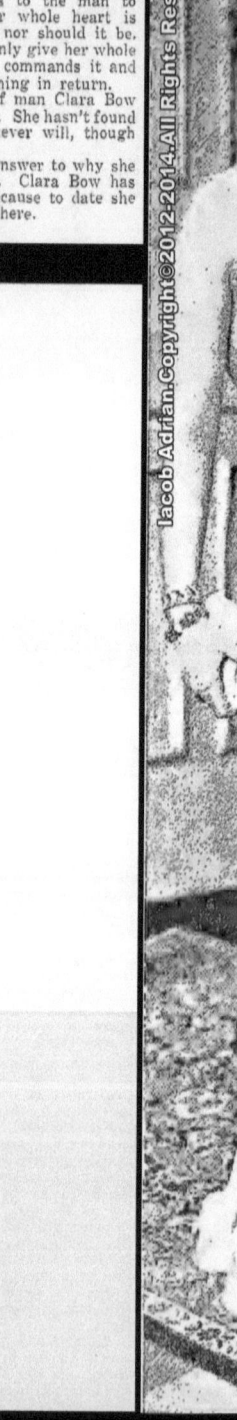

Right this way, ladies and gents, the little lady is about to go into her dance! Clara Bow becomes a most enticing sideshow attraction in Hoopla, her latest talkie which is a picturization of The Barker

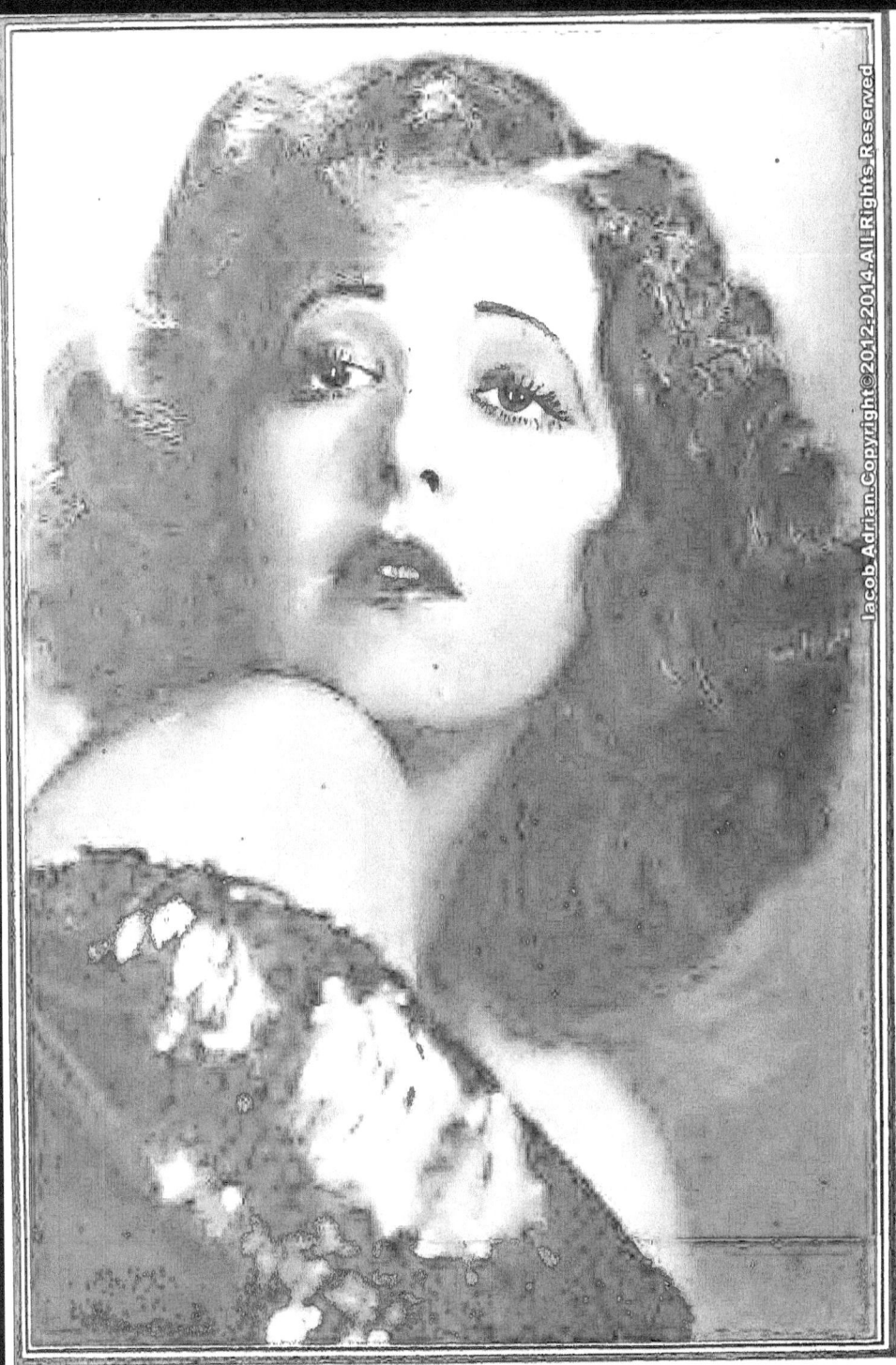

CLARA BOW

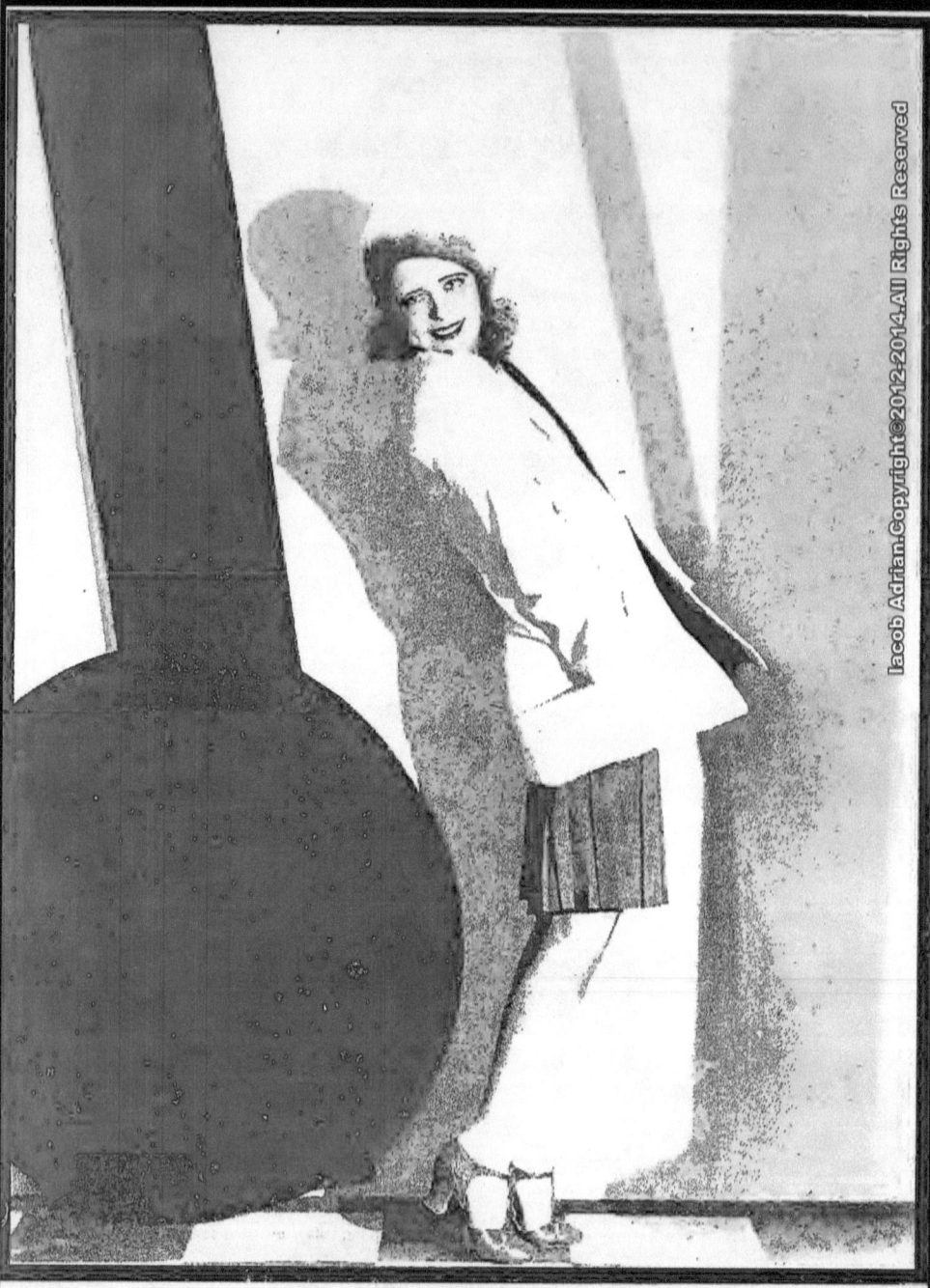

CLARA
BOW

Here the IT girl introduces the latest gasp in the sport fur mode: a jacket of white shaved caracul. With it she wears a red angora tam and a red tweed frock, completing a striking ensemble. You will be interested to know that Miss Bow still leads in national popularity. For the second year in succession, she topped the votes of the country's exhibitors.

ADVENTURES in INTERVIEWING

In which Ruth Chatterton, Clara Bow and Movie Mammas Come under the Study of the Vigorous Mr. Tully

By JIM TULLY

THE most accomplished of the women screen stars I have interviewed is Ruth Chatterton.

A woman of charm and intelligence, she has capacity for life, depth of emotion, and great understanding.

In the opinion of many, among them Jesse L. Lasky, she is the finest dramatic actress in America.

Unusual among people who arrive in Hollywood, she had none of the tribulations leading to eventual success. She was a Broadway star at seventeen.

Miss Chatterton was born in New York City, of American parents with roots in England and France. She was educated in a private school at Pelham Manor.

Accompanied by a chaperon, she and schoolmates spent the Christmas holidays in Washington, D. C. They attended several matinées. Then, at fifteen years of age, she decided to become an actress.

Upon her return to New York, she applied at a theater for work. To her surprise she was given a position in the chorus of a musical comedy. Followed the usual parental objections, and the usual victory for the daughter.

For the next five months she remained with the musical comedy, accepting with a sense of humor tedious rehearsals, dreary hotels, bad food—all the strange manner of life which young ladies in private schools enjoy only vicariously.

During the next season she had the good fortune to be engaged by a stock company which had as featured players Lenore Ulric, Pauline Lord, and Lowell Sherman. All were later to become famous.

ONE of Ruth Chatterton's outstanding qualities is an eagerness to learn. These players taught the young girl the dramatic technique which she was later to develop to a superlative degree.

Several seasons of rigorous training followed, during which she played minor rôles in Broadway productions.

The great chance came when she was chosen as Henry Miller's leading lady in "Daddy-Long-Legs." Her work in this play made her famous.

A year later she was starred in "Come Out of the Kitchen."

At this period J. M. Barrie's popularity in America was at its peak. After Miss Chatterton was co-starred with Henry

Miller in "A Marriage of Convenience," some unkind person decided that she was a "Barrie" type. She appeared in two plays by the whimsical Scotsman, "Mary Rose" and "The Little Minister," and survived both.

Seven years ago, at the pinnacle of her fame, Ruth Chatterton was offered $1,500,000 if she would sign a contract with Mr. Selznick to appear in films for five years.

She did not accept the offer, believing at the time that her best expression was on the stage.

TO refuse three hundred thousand dollars a year is a mistake, unless, of course, some other person offers more. If such an offer was made, Miss Chatterton did not hear it.

When Jim Tully went to interview Clara Bow, she exclaimed, "Sure thing, I've got nothing to hide." Miss Bow, says Mr. Tully, is one of the few women in films who will tell more than the interviewer can use. "Impulsive and straightforward, he says," she is no more subtle than a buzz saw."

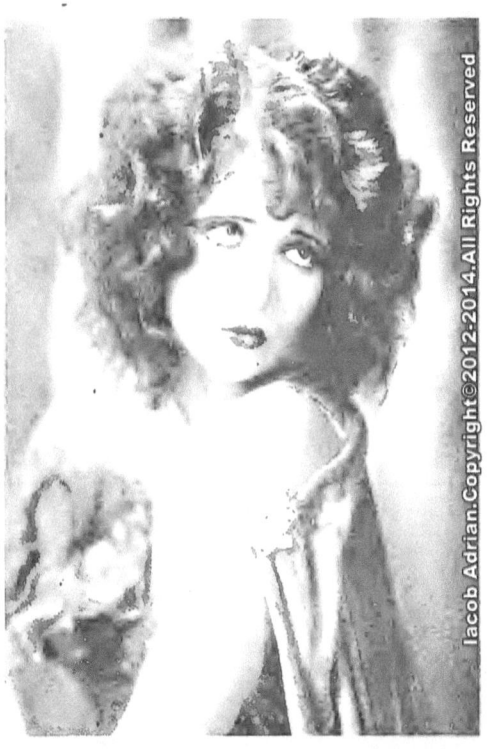

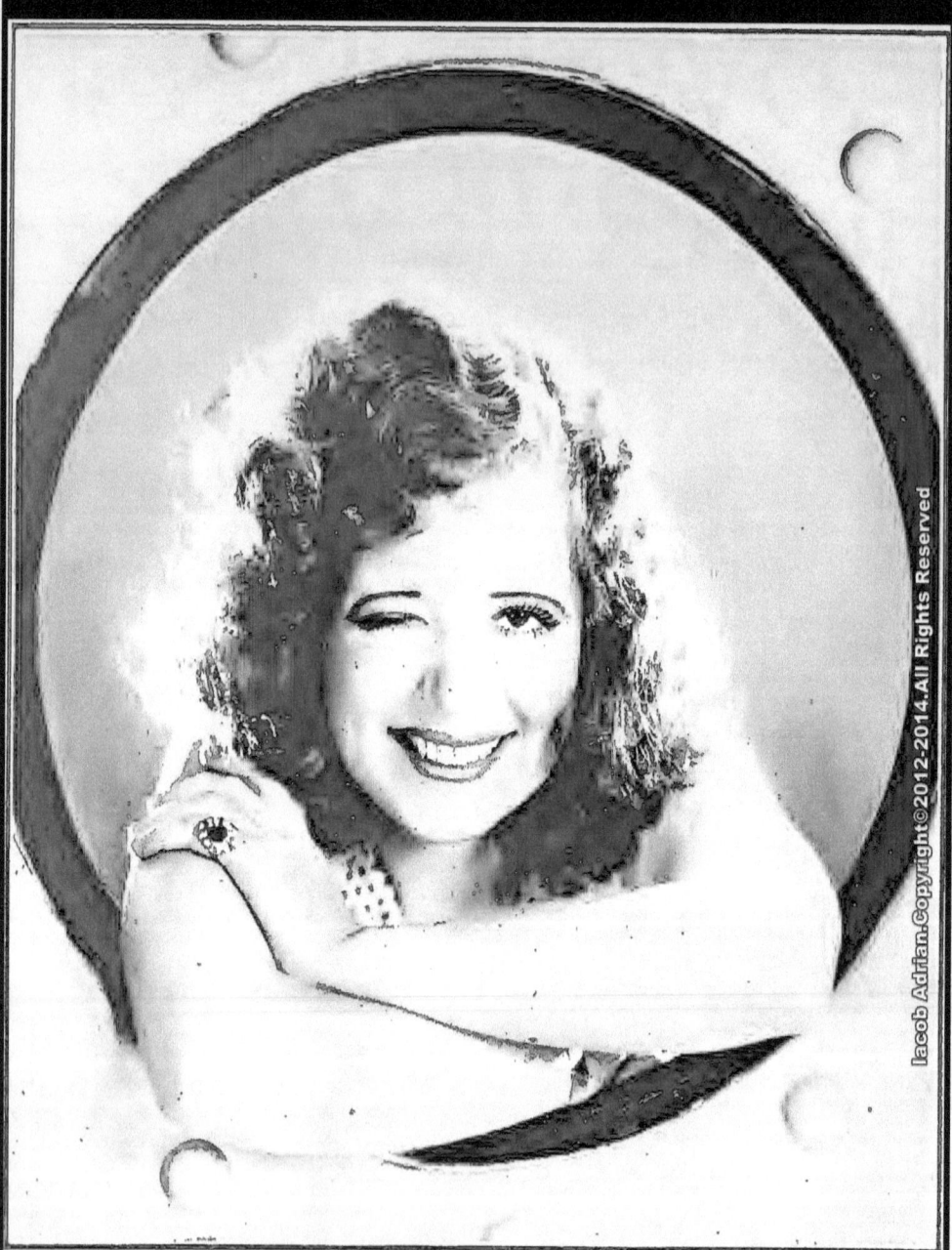

CLARA BOW

You will see a new Clara Bow in her next picture, "True to the Navy." Miss Bow now tips the scales at exactly one hundred and eight pounds. The unveiling of the sylph-like Bow will take place in this newest Paramount film.

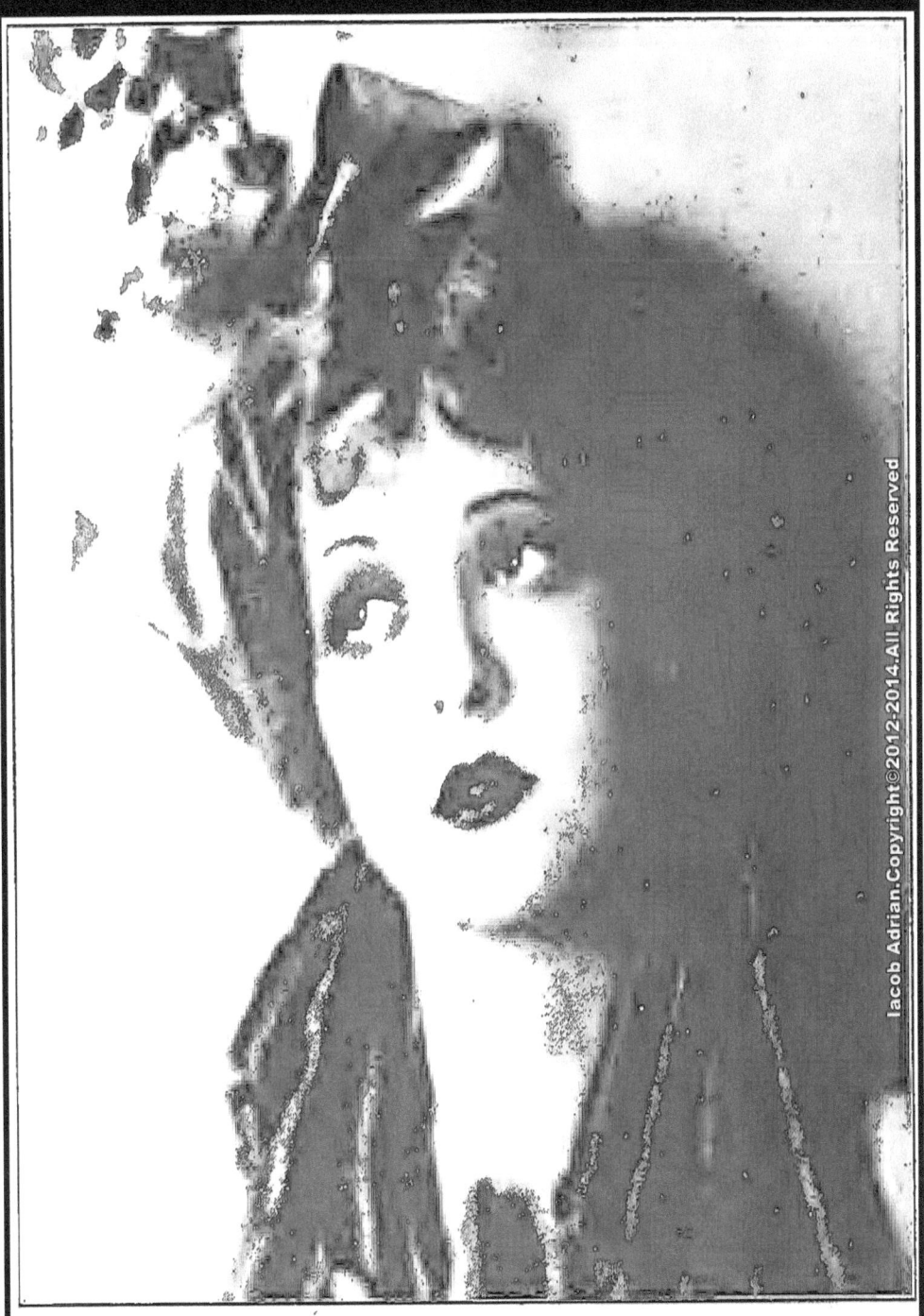

One of the first portraits ever made of Clara Bow.   When this was shot
Miss Bow was playing the hoyden in Elmer Clifton's famous film epic of
whaling adventure, "Down to the Sea in Ships."

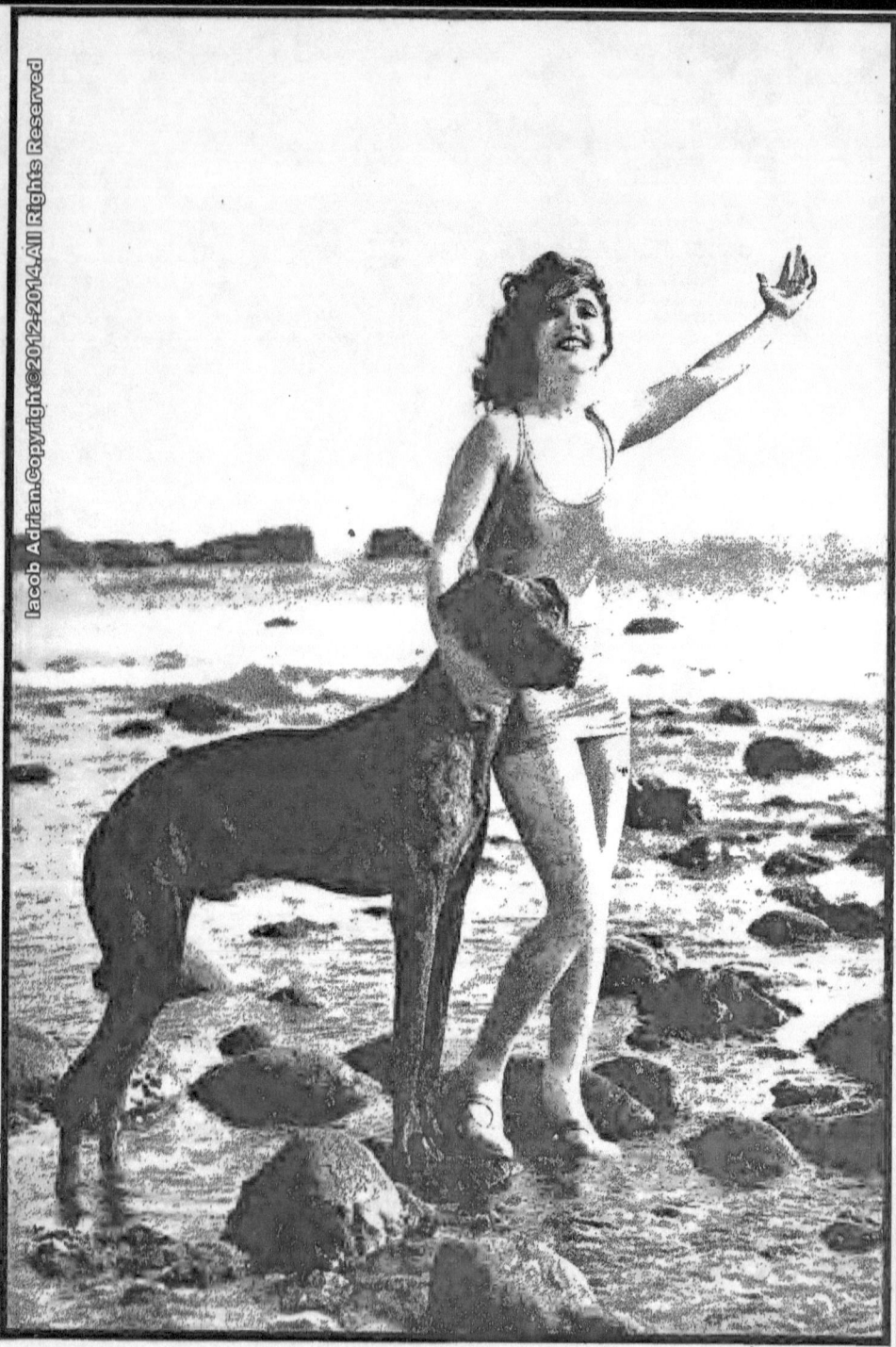

CLARA BOW — The new—and sylph-like Clara—with her newest pet, Duke, a great Dane. Duke goes everywhere with Miss Bow, past no admittance signs and into sound stages where no one ever enters save a star or a director.

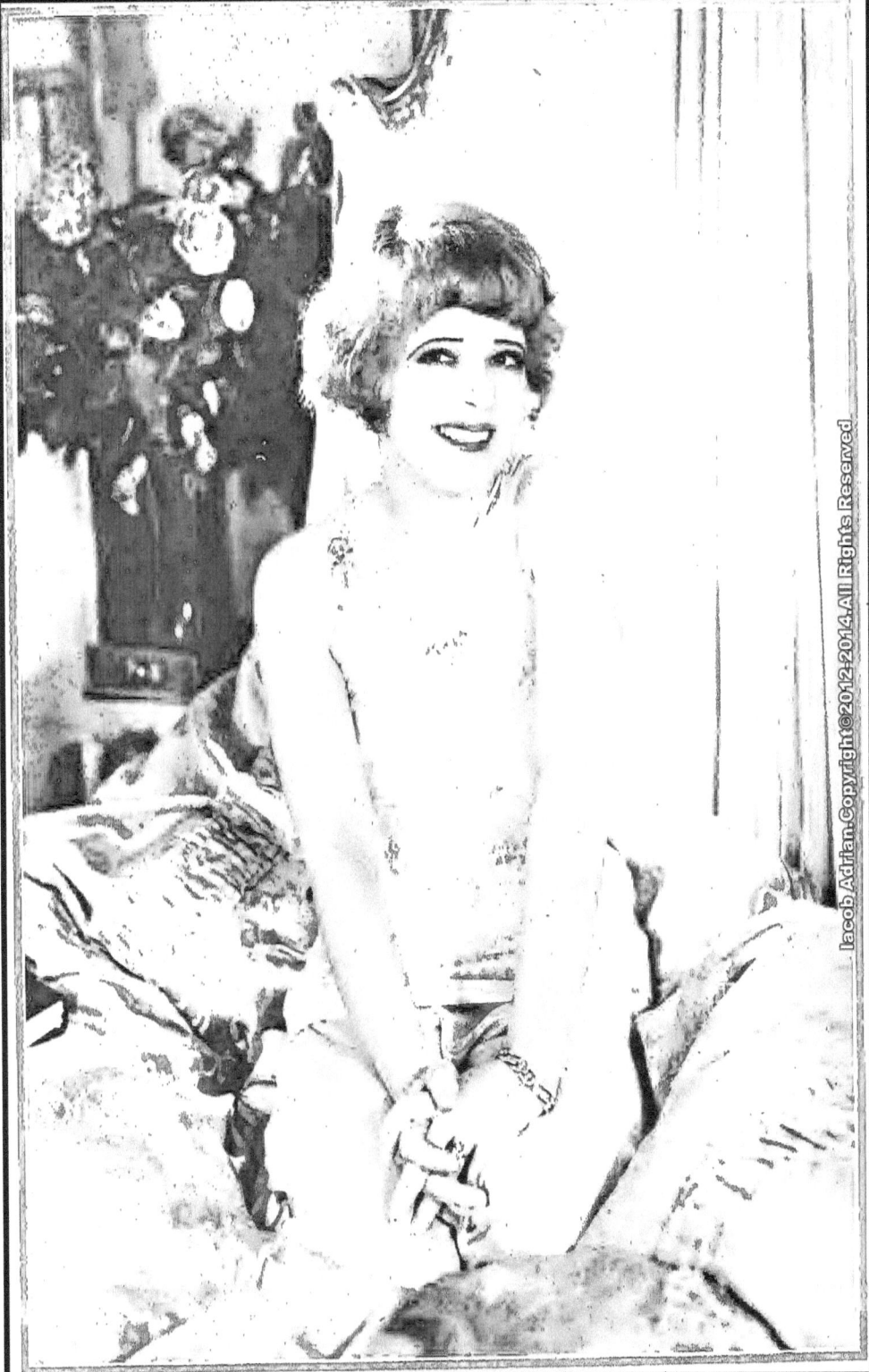

At the right, Miss Bow standing in the arched doorway leading to the dressing room. Rose brocaded curtains, edged with chiffon ruffles and caught back with velvet bands, drape the entrance. The wardrobe is concealed by sliding doors. The carpeting is of a very pale and warm shade of mulberry.

SPECIAL PHOTOGRAPHS
By DON ENGLISH

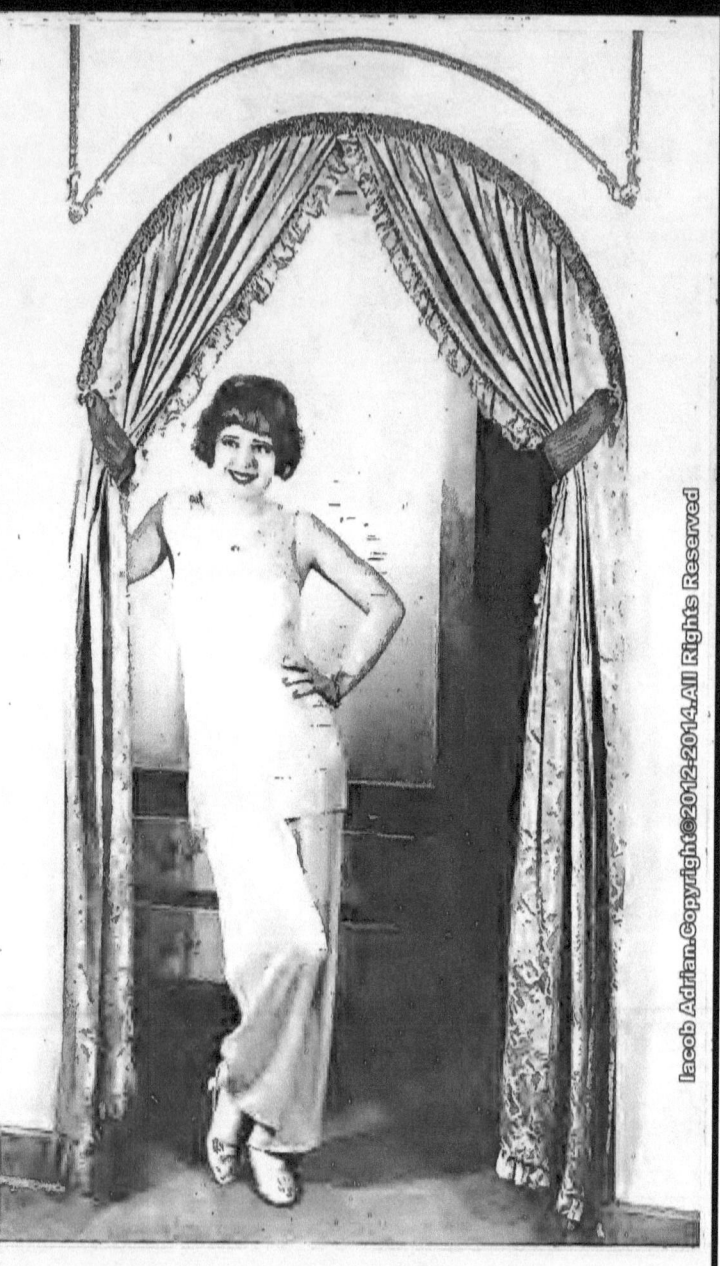

The Bow bedroom is furnished in old ivory enamel. The bed is raised on a dais and covered with a throw of ruck rose brocade. Besides the bed, the boudoir furniture includes a chest of drawers, a dressing table and a writing desk, all in old ivory. The drapes are of antique rose brocade, but the window curtains are of lightly ruffled wisps of maize chiffon, bringing a splash of eternal sunshine into the room. An imported crystal chandelier hangs from the center ceiling.

MOVIE
BOUDOIRS

IV.   CLARA BOW

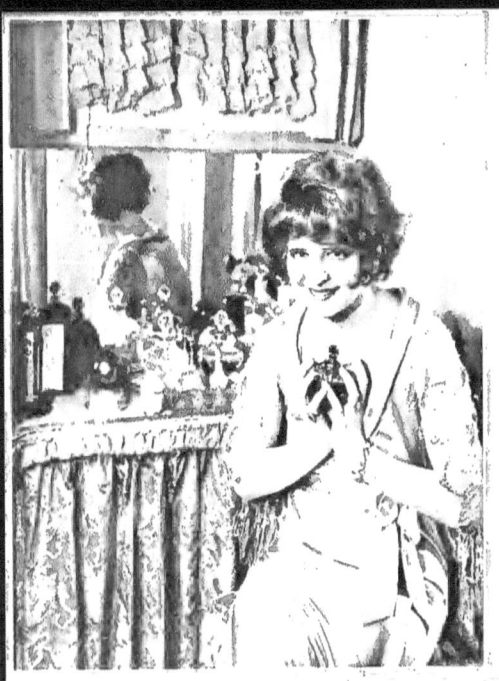

Miss Bow's dressing table is placed beneath a window to permit unobstructed lighting for the intricate details of make-up. This table is draped with the same antique rose brocade that covers the bed and curtains the doorway. The top is covered with glass, over a yellow silk ground. A myriad of perfume bottles are arranged on the table, crystal and onyx vying with jade and different colored quartz.

The Bow boudoir. The star's bed is devoid of footboard or headboard, but is richly draped and covered with generous yards of brocade. Pale rose chiffon, caught into folds and pleats, forms the inner portion of the overhead draping.

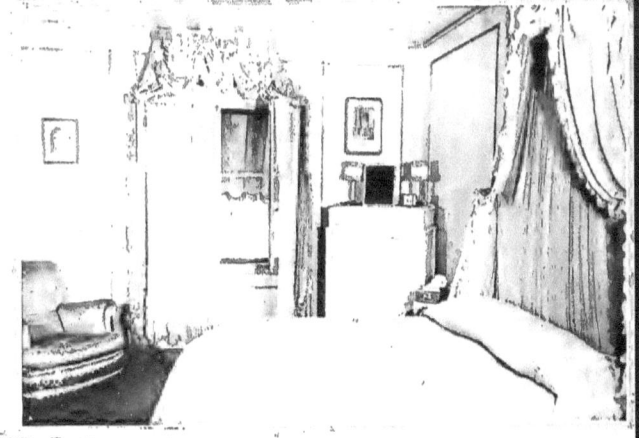

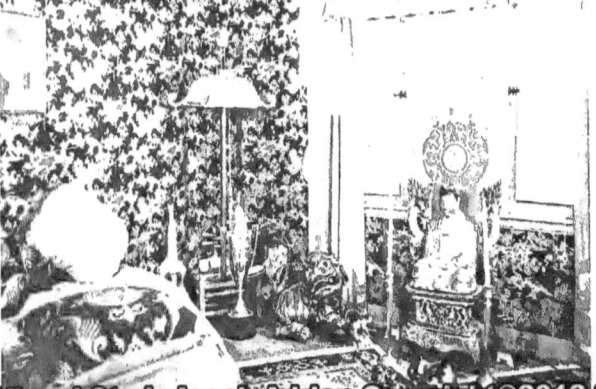

At the left, Miss Bow's Chinese room, designed for relaxation and rest. The walls are covered with a black and gold material, displaying Chinese scenes. One entire corner is devoted to a huge divan that is built into the walls. It is covered with black and decorated with pyramids of red and gold pillows. Red and gold brocade curtains cover the French windows. A black carpet and Oriental rugs conceal the floor. A gold Buddha sits on a throne at one side.

Lilyan Tashman, Marilyn Miller, Evelyn Brent and Grace Moore head the List of Spenders, Their Clothes Budgets Running Over $25,000 Each Year.

in a day her shoes may be changed, not particularly for style, but for comfort and because her feet are her fortune. Marilyn sees that they are comfortable at all times.

Lilyan Tashman has a fondness for shoes: seventy-five pairs at from $14 to $40 a pair brings a shoe bill of $2,000 annually.

MARY NOLAN, while she has many shoes, is fitted readily, and buys her shoes without having them made to order. Her shoe bill is similar to Lilyan Tashman's, though the styles are most simple, and never approach in single items the luxurious golden sandals, for instance, that Miss Tashman wears with an evening gown of Greek influence. Mary prefers the demure pump for evening, and the tie for daytime wear.

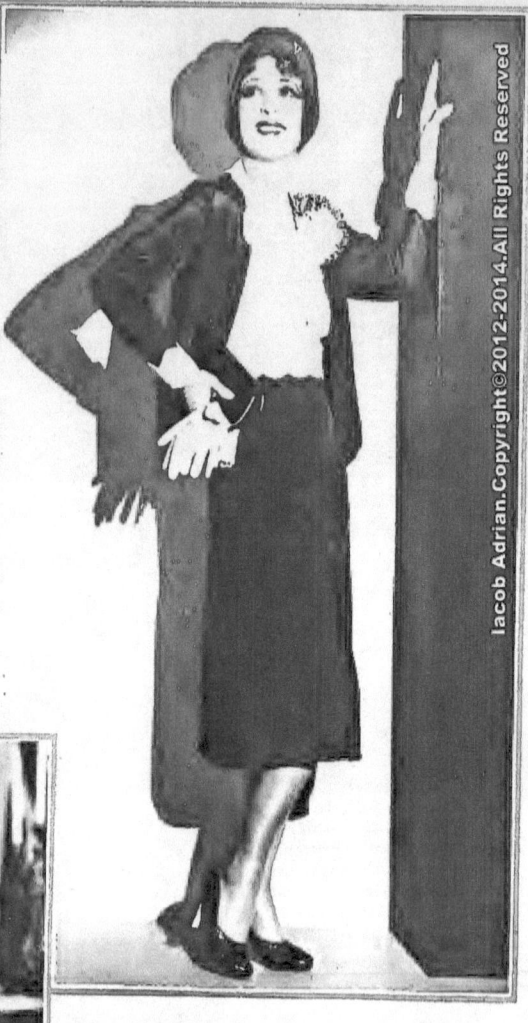

Clara Bow hardly ever looks this dressed up in the afternoon, although she spends $25,000 a year on her wardrobe. This suit is of dark blue crepe, worn with a jaunty blouse of white satin. The shoulder nosegay is of red, white and blue carnations.

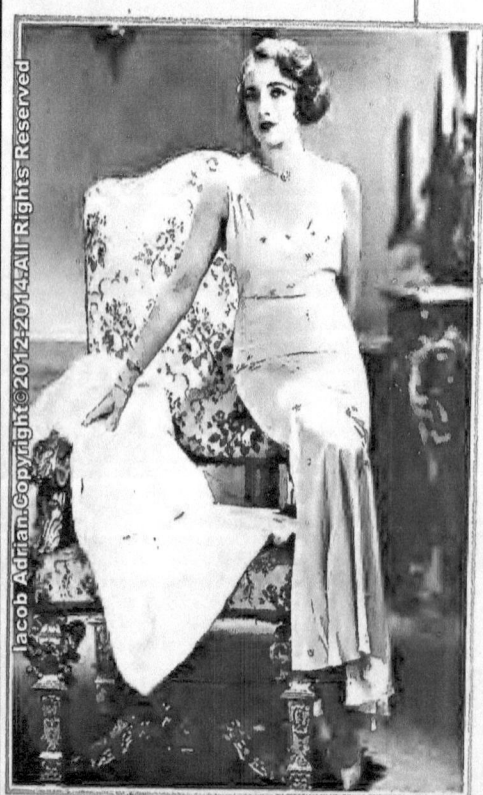

Grace Moore, of the Metropolitan Opera Company and one of Hollywood's own, since she rented an orange ranch to live on and is working with M.-G.-M., buys her daytime shoes and sports shoes at prices from $20 to $25. Thirty pairs of these, and twenty pairs at least of evening shoes at $35 to $40, give her a yearly bill of around $1,500 for shoes.

Jeanette MacDonald, of New York musical comedy background, goes in strongly for shoes. They are a hobby with her. One hundred pairs a year, ranging from sixteen dollars a pair for daytime shoes to twenty-five for evening shoes, gives her a total of shoe money in a year of $2,000. The sight of a slightly

Greer created this simple yet sophisticated velvet gown, sewn with tiny crystal ornaments, for Bebe Daniels. One of Hollywood's wealthiest girls, Miss Daniels believes in dressing conservatively rather than with lavishness.

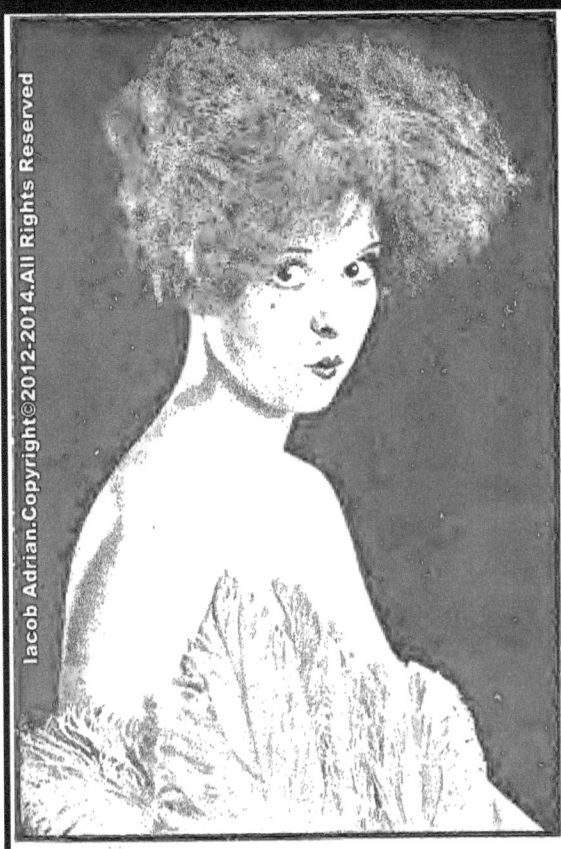

Those Were the DAYS

Clara Bow, as she looked when she first achieved Hollywood. This was after her appearance in "Down to the Sea in Ships" and long before she attracted the attention of the movie millions. The date was 1924, just six years ago. How much happens in Hollywood in six years.

Below, a scene from The Jesse Lasky Feature Play production of "Sweet Kitty Bellairs," produced in 1916 and starring Mae Murray of the bee-stung lips. Miss Murray was a popular star and her performance of the belle of old Bath was looked upon as a scintillating characterization, indeed. "Sweet Kitty Bellairs" was based upon the stage play of David Belasco and Edgerton Castle. It was made into a sound film recently by the Warners.

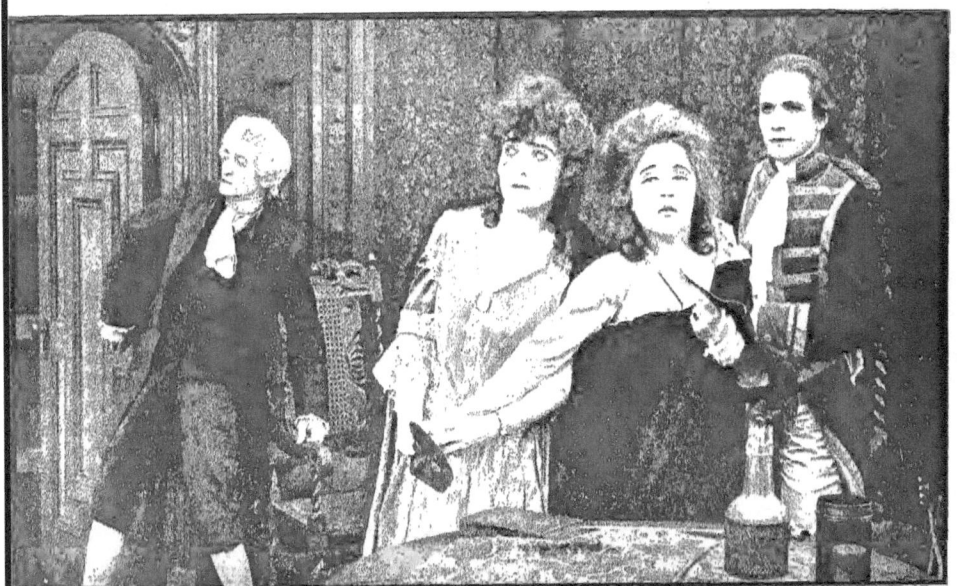

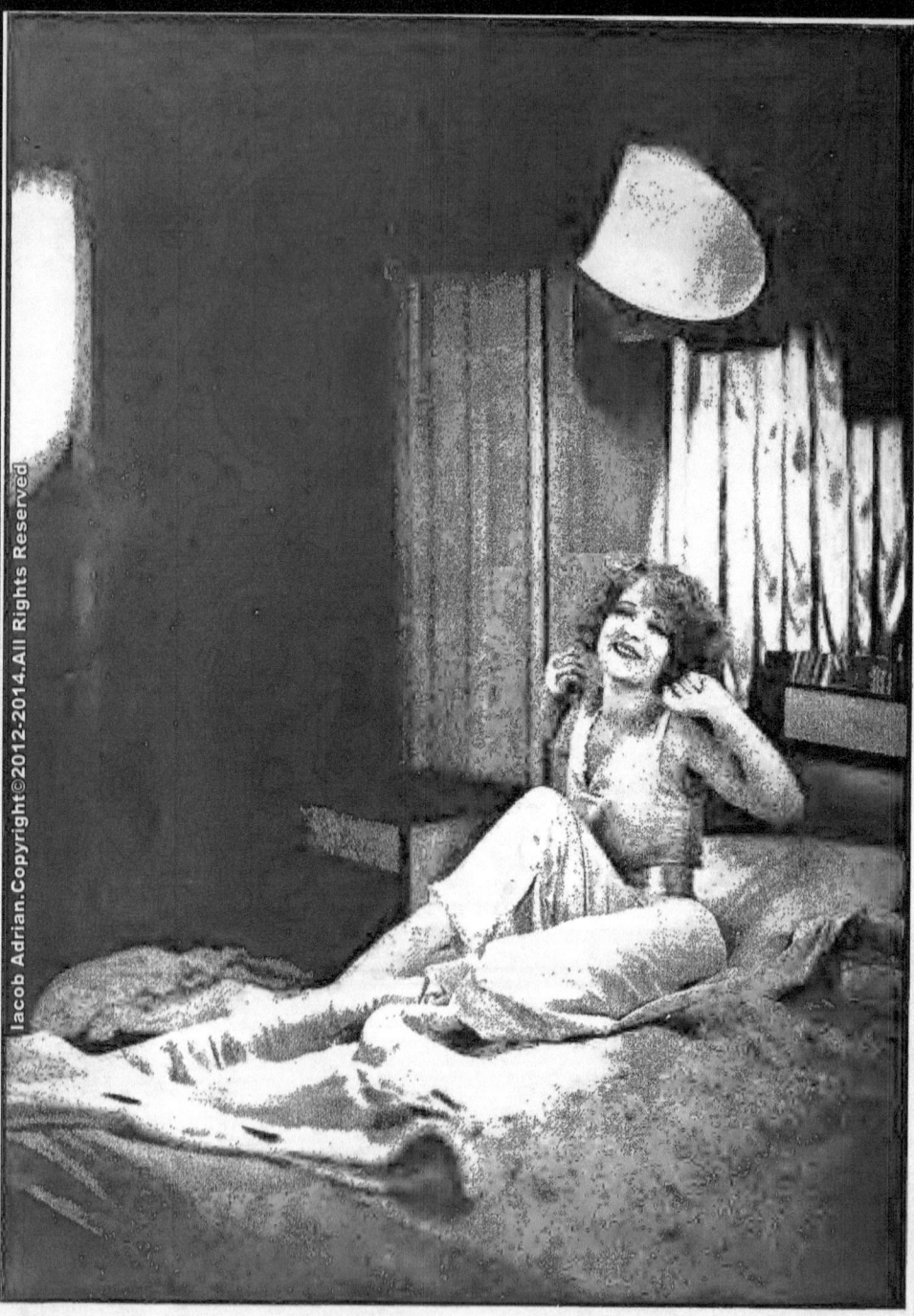

Clara Bow in a scene of her newest talkie, "Her Wedding Night." Miss Bow, says Mrs. St. Johns, always lives in the moment. That came about because she found it necessary to shut out her tragic memories of the past. Those were the terrible recollections of her mother's illness and death and their extreme poverty. Clara Bow has delib- · erately, and with that violent energy of which she is capable, shut the door upon the past. And, because the human mind is so delicate and peculiar a thing, that seems to have closed the door upon the other dimension—the future.

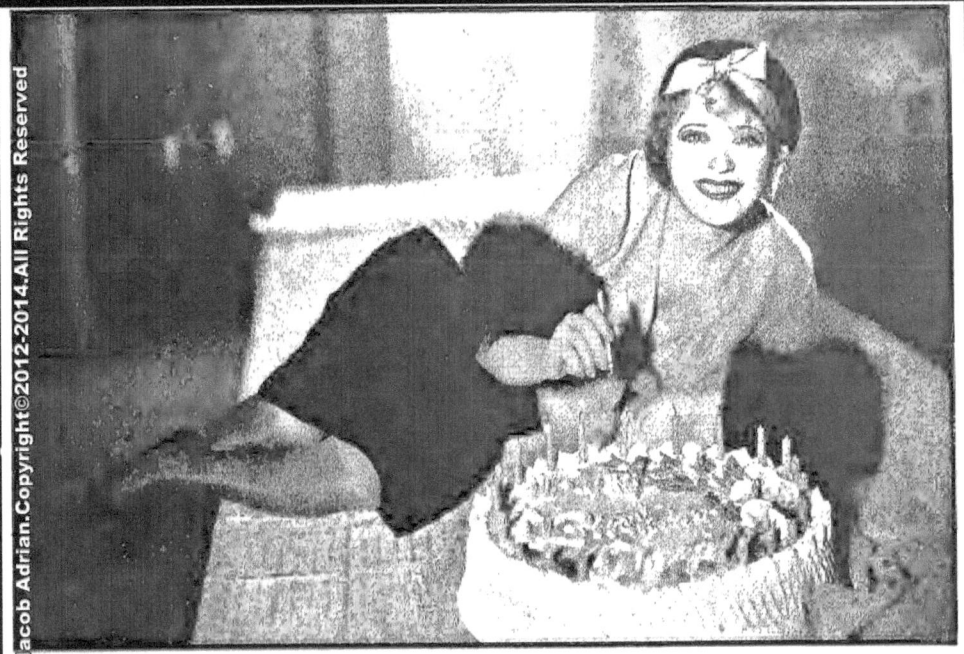

The other day Clara Bow cut her birthday cake at the Paramount studios. It was presented to her by the electricians, the carpenters, the cameramen and others of her technical staff. Miss Bow, you know, is a favorite with the studio employees.

The SALVATION of CLARA BOW

BY
ADELA ROGERS ST. JOHNS

It Will Lie in Her Work, Provided She Gets Real Dramatic Roles with Strength of Characterization

THE difficulty with analyzing Clara Bow is that just as you think you have her safely pigeonholed, she breaks out with something totally at variance, and you have to start all over again.

She can not only change her point of view regarding everything every day, but she can change her whole course of action.

You can never have a very definite viewpoint about things, never a very consistent attitude toward life, until you know yourself thoroughly.

Clara knows no more about herself than she does about the undiscovered tribes of Africa. She has the passionate egotism of youth, which is wholly self-protective and which develops in every very successful youngster in Hollywood as the armadillo develops a shell, but I doubt if she has ever asked herself any very vital questions about her own psychological make-up.

SHE has, you know, more than a touch of mad, Byronic young genius.

The nation has been occupied eternally with her love affairs. The "IT" girl is always in newspaper headlines.

Yet it is my sincere belief that Clara Bow has never been in love. She has had nothing but synthetic imitations. She wants love. Her entire life for years has been surrounded by love, for Clara is one of the few screen stars who has definitely confused her screen personality and her real self. Yet somehow she has never achieved it.

Like a chemist working in his laboratory, Clara goes on experimenting in the laboratory of life, seeking to find love. And every once in a while she gets hold of the wrong combination and the whole works blow up.

The normal human being has a more or less definite balance between the emotional and the mental. The ability to feel and the ability to think. Having a brain doesn't necessarily imply the ability to think. You may own a Rolls-Royce, but if you don't know how to drive it you won't get anywhere.

Almost everyone varies somewhat from the normal in that the balance is stronger on one side than on the other. Clara's ability to feel has been raised to a very

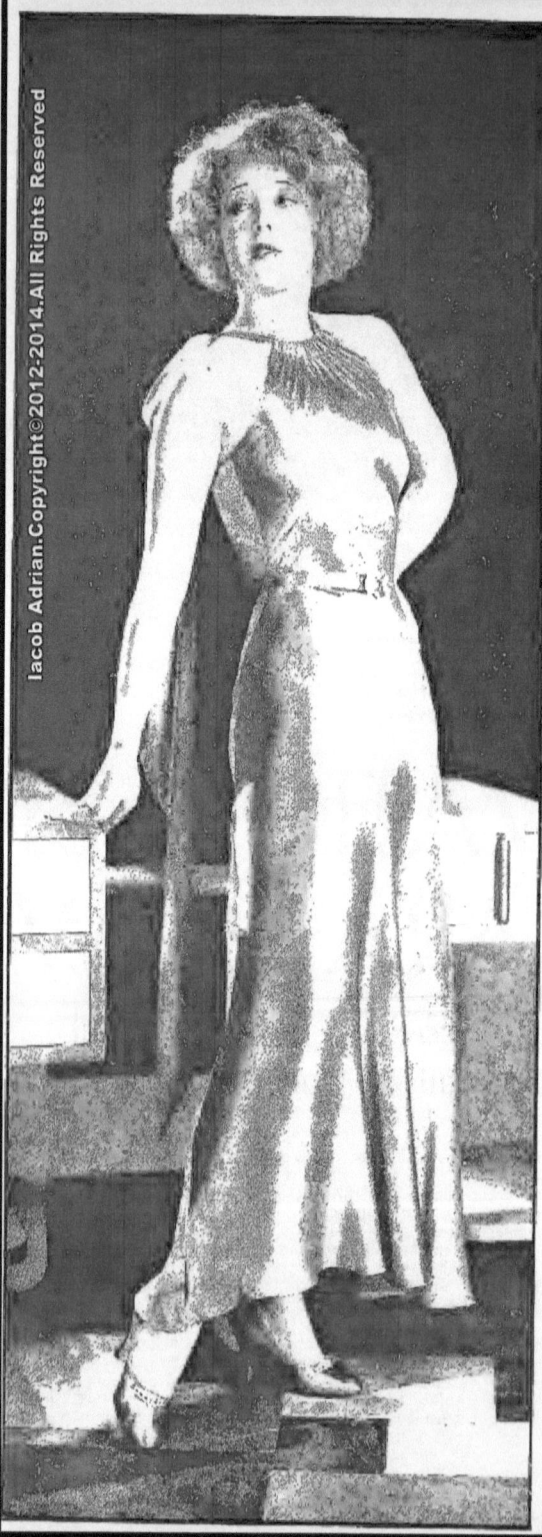

high pitch. But her ability to think hasn't been developed at all.

AFTER all, you cannot ignore Clara. She was at one time the greatest box-office attraction the world has ever known, in that her pictures in one year played to more people than any other pictures have ever done. She should be the greatest dramatic actress on the screen, if Paramount would cease worrying about the Navy and give her stories worthy of her genius. Poor pictures have dimmed the blazing light of her success, but with one real story she would come back as Swanson came back in "The Trespasser."

I have studied Clara Bow closely. I have had opportunity to talk with her for hours. She has always interested me intensely, because, as I say, I honestly believe the girl has genius.

To me, all the strange things about Clara resolve themselves into one amazing fact.

She has limited herself to one dimension of time.

Did you ever stop to think what it would do to you if you actually considered only the present in your every act? If you had no past and no future?

Clara Bow always lives in the moment.

I think that came about because she found it necessary to shut out her memories of the past, if she was to live at all. In fact, at one time when in a fit of terrible depression, she explained to a close friend that when she thought about certain things which had happened in her childhood, she just felt she couldn't go on living.

"THERE was one night in Brooklyn," she said. "It was snowing. My mother and I were cold and hungry. We had been cold and hungry for days. We lay in each others' arms and cried and tried to keep warm. It grew worse and worse. So that night my mother—but I can't tell you about it. Only when I remember it, it seems to me I can't live."

When you force her to talk of those early days, she begins to tremble and grow white.

For some reason, all her memories in those vital childhood years are unbearable. The little boy downstairs, whom she loved and saw burned to death. Her mother's long and desperate mental illness and her tragic death. The day she stood, a poor, emotional, nervous child, and watched them lower the casket that held her beloved mother into a grave.

Why, it happened that even her grandfather, who was her favorite playmate, dropped dead while he was swinging her in a little swing he had made in their tenement room.

Some great writer has said that the memory is the man. To some extent that is true of all of us. Take away memory and we have lost all that has gone to make us what we are.

Yet Clara Bow has deliberately and with that violent energy of which she is capable shut the door upon memory. To save herself, she has locked away the brood of dark and evil memories which were her unfortunate heritage, and has refused to think of herself as having a past.

And because the human mind is so delicate and peculiar a thing, that seems to

The difficulty with analyzing Clara Bow is that, just as you think you have her safely pigeonholed, she breaks out with something totally at variance, and you have to start all over again.

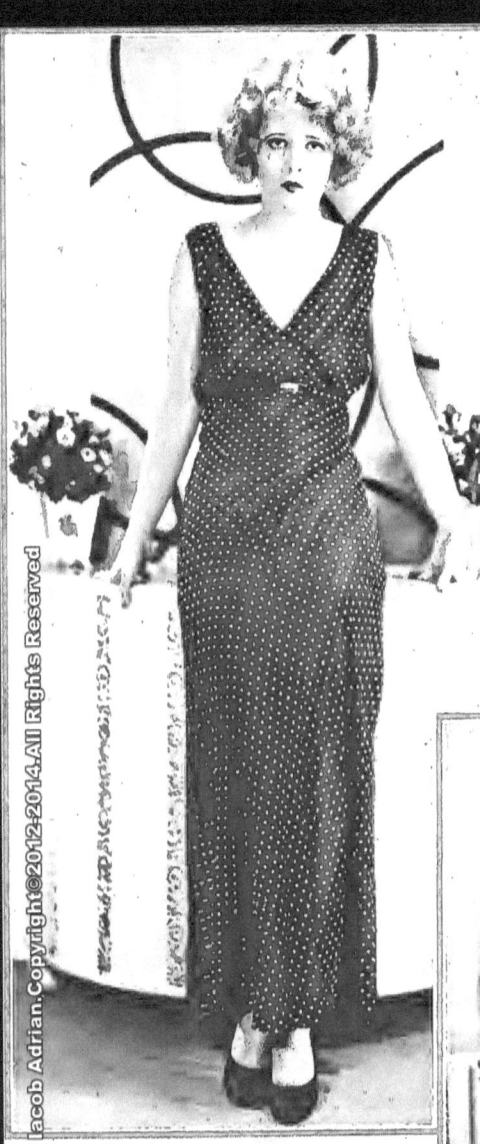

Hollywood Falls Under the Seductive Spell of the Empire Influence

Special Photographs
For NEW MOVIE
by Hurrell and Richee

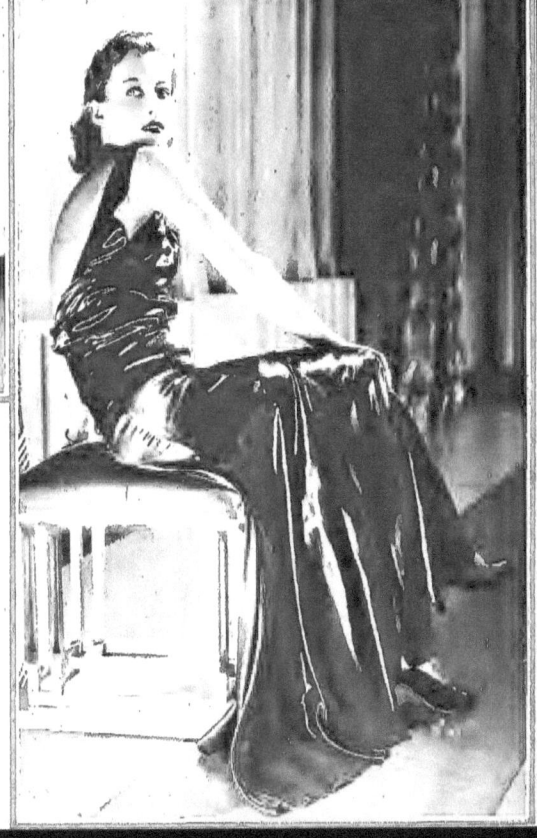

Just above Clara Bow is wearing a chic frock of black crepe, accented with dots of silver and gold in mass design. This high-waisted dress, by the way, is worn by Miss Bow in the restaurant scenes of her new picture, "Her Wedding Night." At the right Joan Crawford is attired in glittering, shimmering satin that gives an appearance of patent leather. This form-fitting evening gown was originated by Adrian expressly for Miss Crawford. Cut in an intricate pattern the dress displays the approved lines for Fall and early Winter evening wear.

When WINTER Comes

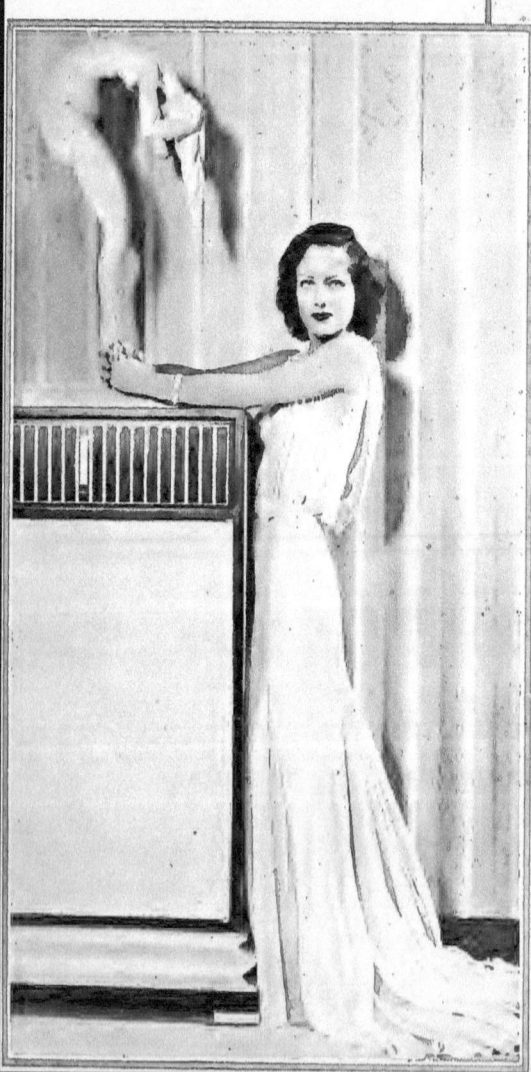

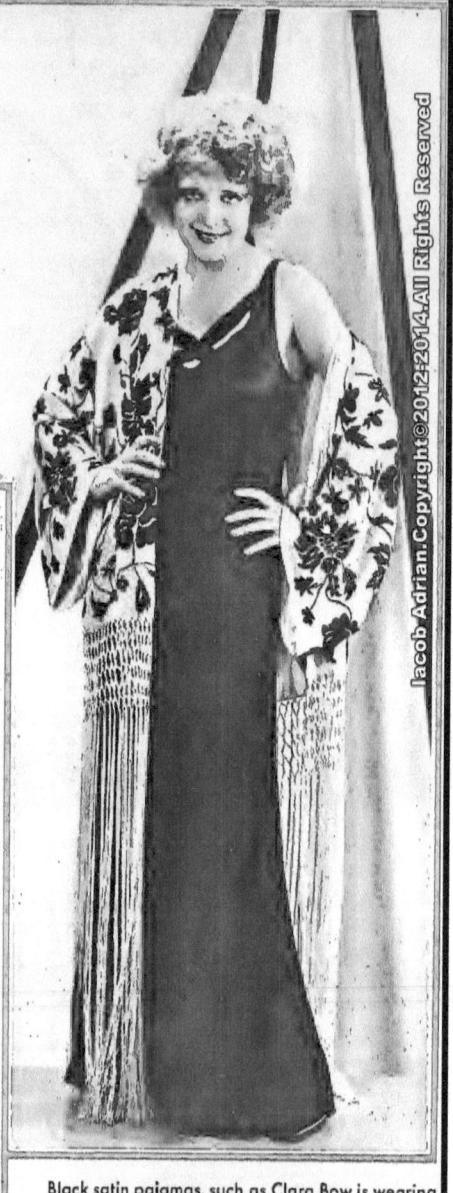

Black satin pajamas, such as Clara Bow is wearing in the picture above, are just the thing for the afternoon in the drawing room. Over the pleated trousers and basque Miss Bow dons a white shawl fringed in white silk and embroidered in black jet. The stunning evening gown worn by Joan Crawford at the left was designed by Adrian. Made of crepe Elizabeth, this gown is fashioned with a slenderizing waistline and curved hipline pattern. The dress ends at the floor in front and has a sweeping train at the back. Beads, hand sewn onto the cowl neckline and adding weight to the drape at the back, lend a delicate richness to the costume, as well as causing weeks of extra work for the costume maker. The wrap worn with this dress is of crepe Elizabeth and is knee length, with flaring sleeves.

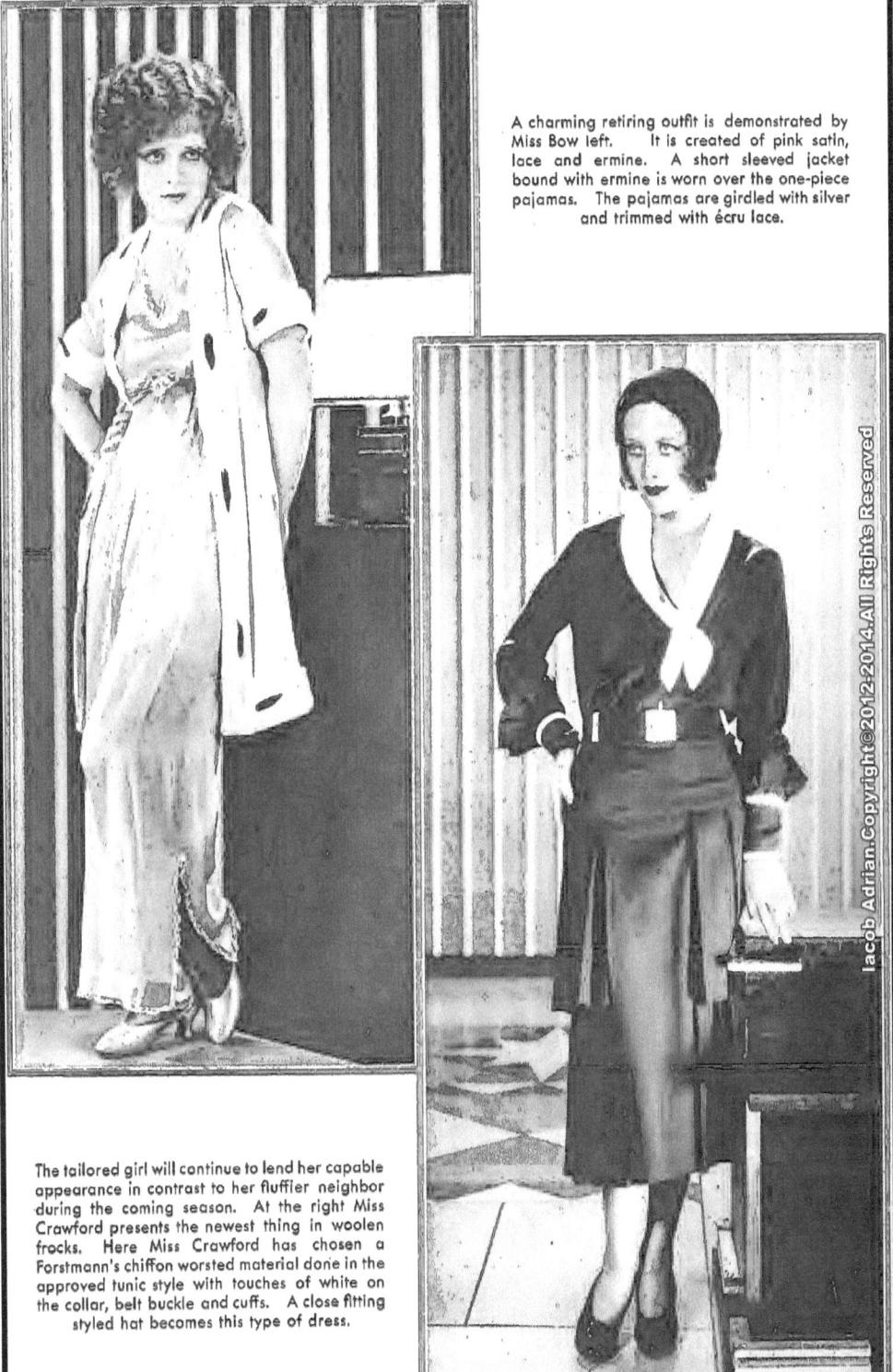

A charming retiring outfit is demonstrated by Miss Bow left. It is created of pink satin, lace and ermine. A short sleeved jacket bound with ermine is worn over the one-piece pajamas. The pajamas are girdled with silver and trimmed with écru lace.

The tailored girl will continue to lend her capable appearance in contrast to her fluffier neighbor during the coming season. At the right Miss Crawford presents the newest thing in woolen frocks. Here Miss Crawford has chosen a Forstmann's chiffon worsted material done in the approved tunic style with touches of white on the collar, belt buckle and cuffs. A close fitting styled hat becomes this type of dress.

The Empire influence again is apparent in the hostess gown worn by Miss Bow at the right. The high waist line, accented with blue velvet ribbon and flowers, allows the narrow pleats of the blue chiffon skirt to fall straight to the floor. A striped metal jacket with jaunty fox-trimmed sleeves gives added effectiveness to the costume.

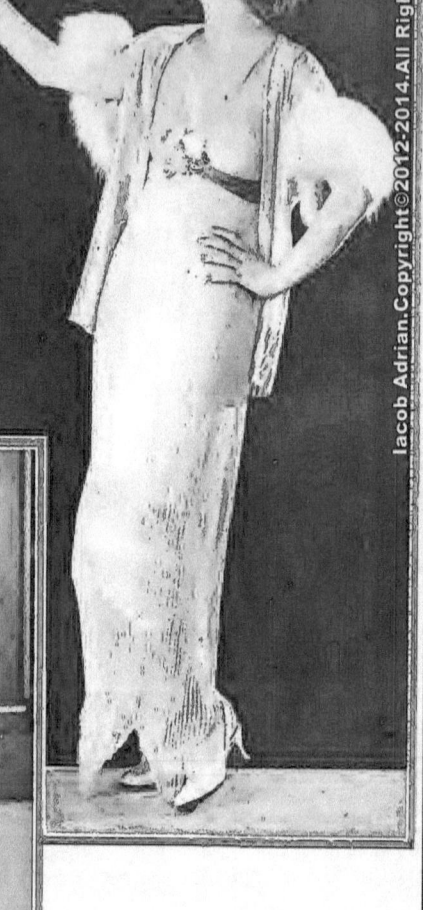

Russia is the inspiration of the smart suit worn by Miss Crawford at the left. Made in the Russian manner of Forstmann's Zenita, a novelty fabric, the suit reveals cartridge trimmings on the sleeves and at the front of the belted-in knee-length coat. All this lends a military air, while the skirt blends with the tailored style.

The Salvation of Clara Bow

have closed the door upon the other dimension—upon the future.

CLARA BOW never looks one moment into the future.

"I don't want to," she told me once. "I don't dare. I distrust the future. If someone would lift the veil for me, I wouldn't let them. It is better not to look ahead and not to look back. I —*will* not look back. I must not. And I dare not look ahead. I am afraid."

So we find her living only in the moment, only in the present. Can't you see how that must change every action? The whole balance and accustomed values of life are destroyed.

Of course, that is what makes her a very great actress. Since only the moment has reality, her acting becomes intensely real to her. She is so glad to get away from reality that her parts seem real to her. She loves to have them seem real. Her greatest joy is in her work, when she is being someone else, living vicariously, getting away from herself and being some girl whom she would much rather have been.

The drama of a love affair, of men, is another escape from that reality, an escape we may all crave at times, but Clara more than anyone, because reality has shown her so much horror. The passion and excitement of a love affair—and in Clara's mind a love affair is about fifty per cent of each— are intense enough to hold her vitally in the present.

It also does another thing. It keeps her from being alone. And she simply *will* not be alone, ever, even for a moment. Those quiet hours which most of us crave, when we can take stock of ourselves, when we can rest and read and think things out, are not for Clara. She doesn't want to think. She must occupy herself with something outside, something definite all the time. Naturally, a love affair is the perfect answer to that.

SO Clara has had a long list of them. And in this connection it isn't possible to forget that her plastic mind, living so vitally in the present, has accepted the estimate of herself as the "It" girl.

There was Gilbert Roland, Gary Cooper, Vic Fleming and a few others. But they always seemed surface things to me. It will take a very strong man to break through Clara's shell of self-centered egotism, her fears and fancies about life. That fear makes her pull back, hesitate to allow anyone to enter too deeply into her heart.

Then, when you live in the moment, you must tire of things very quickly. So much of enjoyment, of permanence is built upon memories and anticipation. Clara has neither.

Clara met Harry Richman. She was jockeyed into the engagement. No matter what comes, I think it would be only fair of Mr. Richman to let Clara keep the $10,000 diamond. He surely had more than $10,000 worth of publicity from his engagement to the "It" girl. However, they grew very fond of each other. Then Clara got a little tired of Richman, too. The big kick of a love affair to Clara is its beginnings. That is true of many women. Beginnings and endings embody the most drama. The most excitement. That is why Clara seeks them.

Rex Bell, a stalwart and handsome young cowboy, was seen about with her for a time.

You see, Clara Bow doesn't do these things from any inner conviction, with any courage to live up to her own beliefs. She has no inner convictions— only warm-hearted impulses. She acts entirely upon these. They are often honest, often generous, often emotionally terrific, but they are sometimes unwise.

Now all this is important only for one reason. It is childish to be sentimental about people, to start attempting to help them, even to discuss their mental processes, unless they belong to your actual orbit, or unless they belong to the universal orbit.

I believe that Clara Bow as an artist is being menaced by her uncontrolled actions. None of us wants to see the waste, the tragedy, of a Barbara La Marr, a Mabel Normand, to happen again.

If her work were big enough to absorb that surplus of nervous energy, that tremendous vitality, for which she now finds outlet in the excitement of men and synthetic love affairs; if her emotional force could by some engineer, dealing in human power instead of forces of nature, be turned into the proper channel of her art, Clara might contribute great things to the theatrical history of our generation.

I BELIEVE her capable of reaching heights as an actress not yet reached by anyone in pictures. Her day as a mere personality, as the "It" girl, is over. But in its place, were she given proper stories, proper direction, would be found the day of a great dramatic actress.

Clara is a hard worker. Loves to work, will work, any hours, under any conditions. Work would be her salvation. Not these silly little parts which she can do without expending one-tenth of her powers. But real parts that demand finesse, strength, characterization. In a new tempo, and a new medium, but such parts as made Bernhardt and Duse famous.

There is a feeling that the public would not accept Bow in anything but "It" rôles. I believe that the public will accept fine work and good strong drama from anybody. I believe no great artist on the screen can fail of a public, if given suitable vehicles.

Art is always above personality. We are concerned with Clara Bow as an artist. And upon her chance as an artist depends her salvation as a person.

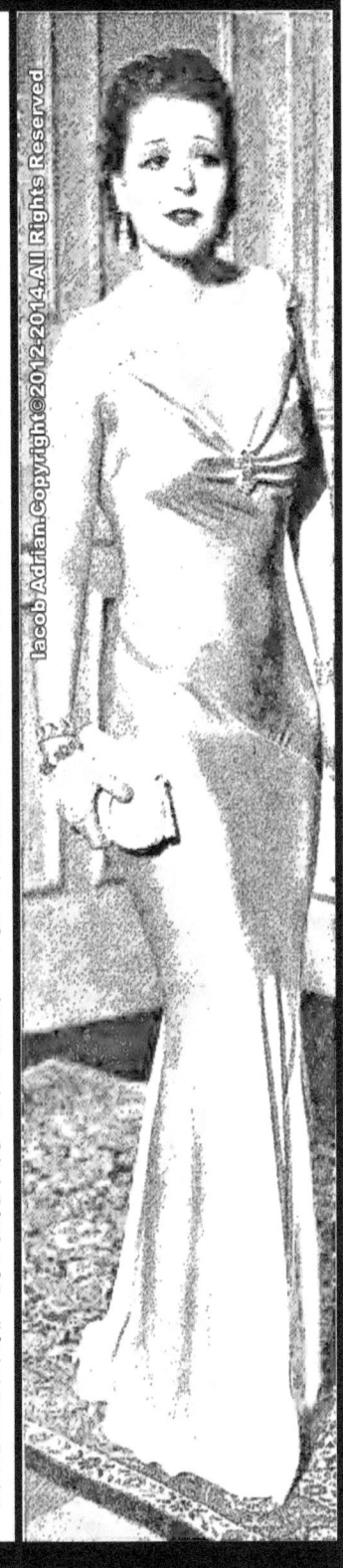

The Screen's SEARCH for BEAUTY

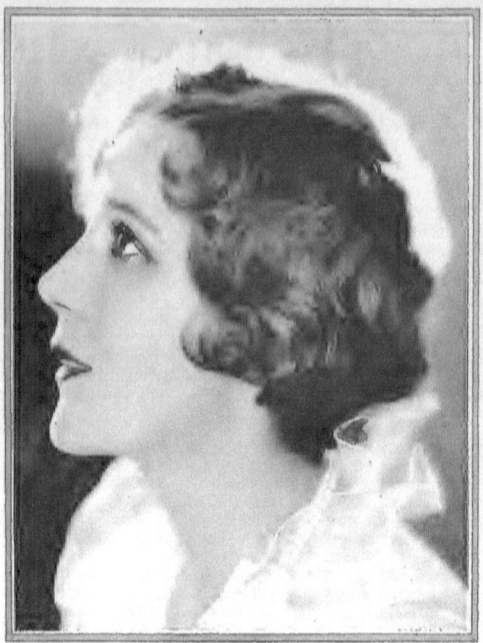

By ADELA ROGERS ST. JOHNS

Mary Pickford's beauty is physical and evident. Her face is camera perfect. On no matter what basis you estimated the beauties of the screen, "America's Sweetheart" would have to be included. It is her peculiar power to stir certain feelings that gives her a special kind of beauty.

MARY PICKFORD'S beauty is physical and evident. Her face is camera perfect. Out of a sitting of photographs which includes twenty or thirty negatives, Mary will have to discard only one or two—and those usually because of some fault in lighting. On no matter what basis you estimated the beauties of the screen, "America's Sweetheart" would have to be included.

But it is her peculiar power to stir certain feelings that gives her a special kind of beauty.

For some reason—perhaps it is the contour of her face—Mary is ornamented by our own sweetest memories. She touches the strings of our treasures, the treasures we don't talk about.

The first time we read the story of Lancelot and Elaine. The first time we heard some beloved song. A first kiss. A moonlight night in—Carmel, or Lake Geneva, or Central Park. The lace wedding veil hidden away in a cedar chest in the attic. A young mother bending above her first-born.

Bootleggers and prohibition, gangsters and lipsticks, haven't destroyed the yearning for romance, for sweetness, for gentle goodness, that persists century after century, and in every place.

The woman who can supply that need has beauty. Whether she is sixteen or sixty, whether her face meets all or none of the physical requirements of the immortal Helen—that woman has beauty.

I remember one time being introduced to a girl about whose beauty a mutual boy-friend had told me much. Frankly, I was staggered when I saw her. It

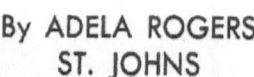

"It wasn't Mary Pickford's face alone that made her the most famous of all stars. It was a beauty that could rest, comfort, satisfy the tired longing in many tired people. You can't get that beauty in beauty parlors." — ADELA ROGERS ST. JOHNS.

seemed to me that I had never encountered a plainer face. Yet I knew that the boy had been perfectly sincere.

A year or two later, I found myself telling someone else how beautiful this girl was. I meant it. You see, in the meantime I had grown to know her.

That kind of beauty lasts. Unless it is destroyed by some pretensions of youth, it is ageless.

Not long ago I was at a house party given by Marion Davies. There were a number of the most beautiful young girls in pictures at the table. My seat was next to that of a man famous on two continents as an explorer and scientist—an adventurous, daring, hard-living man of the great world. Never having met him before and not wanting to start on his trips into unknown lands, I asked him which woman there he thought the most beautiful.

"How could I tell?" he said "I don't know any of them."

"But you can see them all," I said.

He looked. "I suppose they are beautiful," he said, at last, "but will you think me ungallant if I say I do not see beauty in any face here except Miss Davies'? They are like lamps without a light inside."

LATER, when we became better acquainted, he showed me a picture of his wife, who he said was the most beautiful woman he had ever seen in all his travels. I don't think, really, he knew anything about how she looked. Even I, just looking at the picture once, could see why he thought her beautiful.

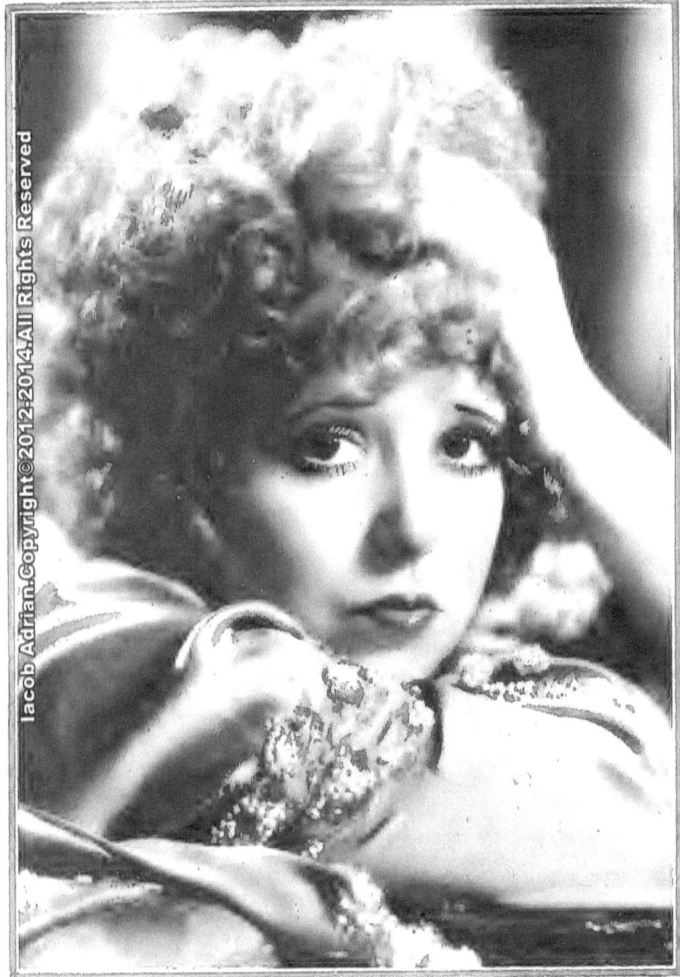

Photograph by Gene Robert Richee

Clara Bow is a living symbol of our idols—speed and pep. She moves all the time. When, in any picture, do you ever see Clara still? Then, too, she has a thing we all prize highly, youth. Real youth. She must have been born with a fund of nervous energy that would run the dynamo of an electric plant.

You don't get that kind of beauty in beauty parlors, Paris dress salons, gymnasiums. You get it by high thinking and clean living. You get it by unselfishness and charity. Which still pay dividends, even in the world of screen beauty.

Even when Mary is a little devil, even when she's a vixen and a termagant, she still has that face which suggests beauty of soul. You can't get away from it.

JANET GAYNOR has much the same thing, though in a little different channel. Janet is the romance of life. The girl for whom knights battled. Her physical aspect also awakens a definite and unusual emotional response. You look at her, you do not think particularly whether she is beautiful or not. But you want to rescue her, protect her.

Mary and Janet are our romantic beauties of the screen.

It isn't, you know, a bad idea. Even in fashions, we have had to come back in some respects to the romantic.

Marguerite Clark was the Janet Gaynor of her day. The doll you couldn't bear to see handled by careless hands. Mae Marsh, too, had the ability to awaken quick and loving feeling—that was her beauty, though in truth she was a plain little person. The lamp was lighted within, always. Its glow drew you, made you love her.

I wonder if, in the last analysis, anything that awakens love isn't beautiful.

THERE is another screen beauty who has a typically modern appeal. She is a beauty today, a great beauty in popular estimation, yet I doubt if she would have been called beautiful in other ages. Clara Bow.

She looked so good, so kind, so true, so—oh, as if she'd always understand, always be there in the pinches.

It wasn't alone Mary Pickford's pretty face, her charm of personality, that made her the most famous of all stars.

It was a beauty that could rest, comfort, satisfy the tired longing of many tired people. Probably they weren't conscious of it, probably they never analyzed it. But you can't overthrow human nature in a few short years of freedom and license. Woman has been for centuries a part of religion, a part of spirituality. Upon her breast, man has sought surcease from burdened existence.

Mary suggests that Woman. The little Mother. James Whitcomb Riley's "The Girl I Loved."

They call her the "IT" girl.

Short, to the point, goes well in headlines and twenty-four sheets.

But I don't think Clara's beauty is merely that of sex. After all, sex is biological and, as the great and sedate Plutarch once remarked, "All women are fair when the candles are out."

This is distinctly an age of speed, of movement. We love fast motion. Our dances of the past few years—the Black Bottom, the Charleston, the Varsity Drag, the Shimmy, have all been rapid movement.

Our lives are a succession of going quickly from one place to another, one thing to another, and our great national idol of the moment is the man who went farthest fastest—Colonel Lindbergh.

Sports have speeded up terrifically. Records on

Romantic Beauties of the Motion Picture Screen

the track are seconds faster than they were a decade ago. Baseball is speedier. Football has developed speed and forward passes—faster, more open than the games of a few years past.

Trains, boats, automobiles — everything is speed and movement.

All that speed Clara Bow represents in a girl.

SHE has the national quality—pep. We adore pep. She moves all the time. When, in any picture, do you ever see Clara still? Her eyes sparkle with an inward fire, which is another outward sign of an inward pep.

It isn't just the beauty of graceful motion. That can be slow. Clara has all the beauty of a very fast thoroughbred horse. Whether she does the modern dance that we think fascinating, every movement suggests that she might start it at any moment.

A symbol is Clara Bow. A symbol of our idols, speed and pep.

Many young girls of today have that beauty. Clara does less than nothing to keep hers. She must have been born with a fund of nervous energy that would run the dynamo of an electric plant. Or perhaps it is because she doesn't exercise or bother about her looks that she manages to keep up that terrific pace of hers.

Clara takes care of her looks by fits and starts—a good deal the way most young girls do. For two or three days, she has massages, puts on her cold cream every night and rubs her face with a piece of ice every morning. Then for a week, she forgets all about it.

Again, Clara has a thing that we prize highly—youth. Real youth. It is her problem now to approach thirty, as distinctively, as stunningly as Swanson or Norma Talmadge.

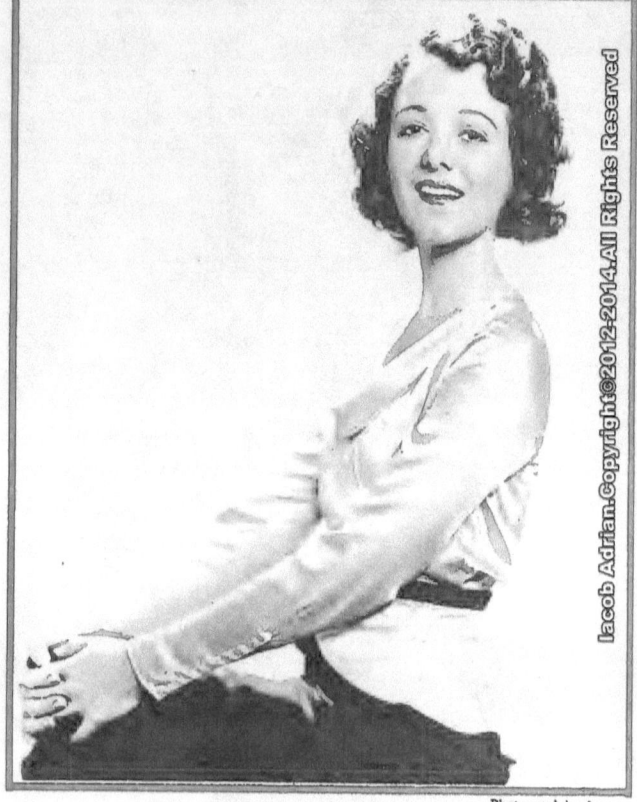

Photograph by Autrey

Janet Gaynor is the romance of life, says Mrs. St. Johns. Her physical aspect awakens a definite and unusual emotional response. You look at her, you do not think particularly whether she is beautiful or not. But you want to rescue her, protect her.

I sometimes wonder if men don't prefer prettiness to beauty. There is a fragile, feminine, lovable quality about prettiness that beauty doesn't have. Sometimes great beauty creates a feeling of awe. Prettiness does just the opposite.

Pretty women are pettable—if there is such a word. And they have a gayety, a lightness which I love.

"A pretty little woman" still has a good deal of an edge on most of her sex.

THE prettiest woman on the screen is Marion Davies. There were shots of her in that delightful picture "The Florodora Girl" that were prettier than anything else I have ever seen in pictures.

She has every true element of prettiness. Divine dimples. Little golden freckles on her pert, uptilted nose. Curly blond hair. Wide blue eyes. Even, white teeth. Big blue eyes with black lashes that curve back and are tipped with gold.

She knows how to make the most of it, too. Probably her clothes are smart and up to the moment in fashion. But they are always pretty clothes. I have never seen her attempt the striking, the ultra, the severe. Her dinner gowns are soft blues and exquisite orchids and very pale pinks.

Her hats always have a little softly curved brim.

Her sweaters are woolly ones, of angora, with adorable woolly collars. She is essentially dainty in every little appointment.

And she has the prettiest laugh in the world.

Most pretty women are blondes, have you ever noticed that?

Mary Miles Minter was one of the prettiest girls who ever won stardom. And I wonder if you remember Wanda Hawley? There was a scene in the prologue of that great picture made by Cecil De Mille, "Old Wives for New," in which Wanda, dressed in a gingham apron, came down to a little stream. I will never forget that.

THERE are a lot of pretty girls on the screen today. Jean Arthur, Loretta Young, Leila Hyams, Joan Bennett, Laura La Plante, Joan Marsh, Jeanette MacDonald.

In fact, unless you have something to go with prettiness—such as Marion Davies' great comedy talent or Mae Murray's dancing and instinct for the picturesque—you don't get above the level of a good leading woman.

June Collyer is pretty, but she must watch herself for the affectation of a set smile that is becoming almost as objectionable as Buddy Rogers' omnipresent dental ad.

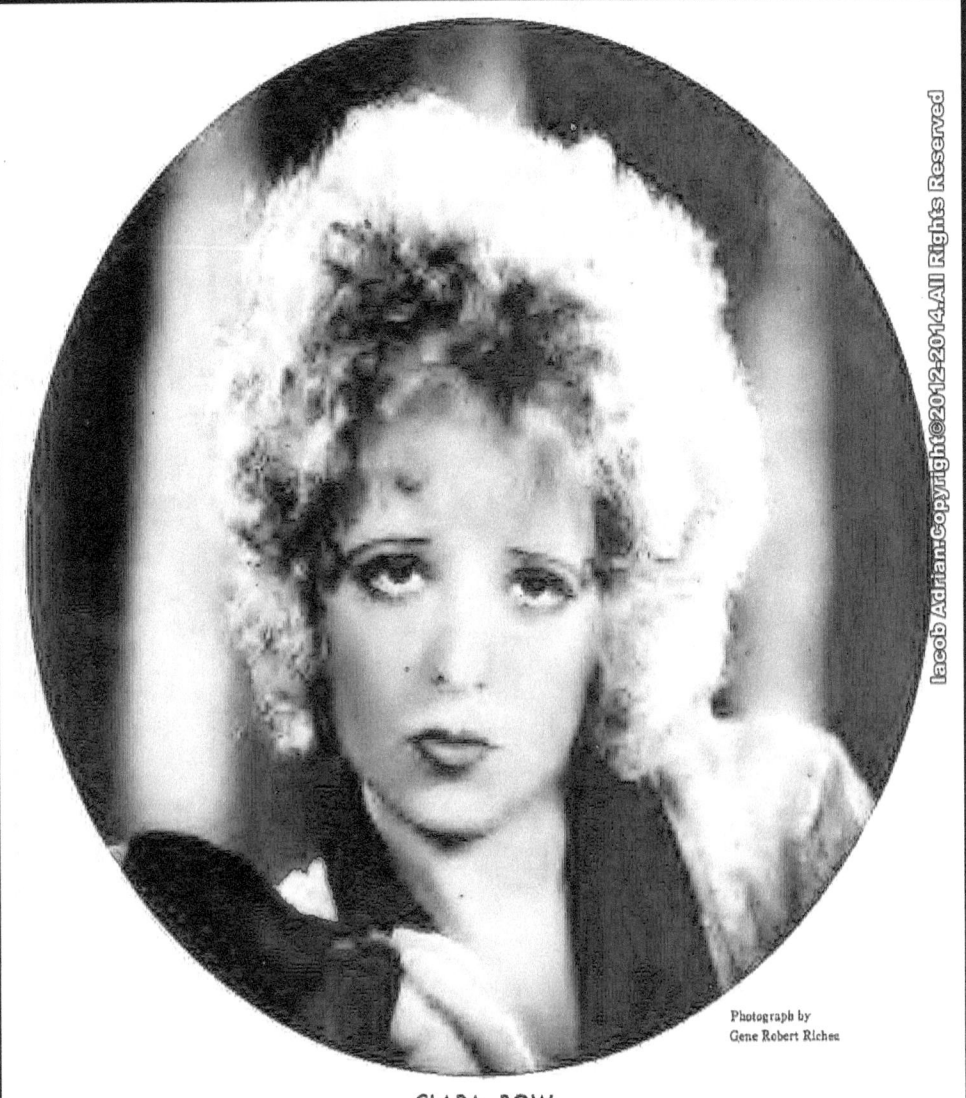

Photograph by
Gene Robert Richee

CLARA BOW

Gallery
of
Famous
Film Folk

The
New Movie
Magazine

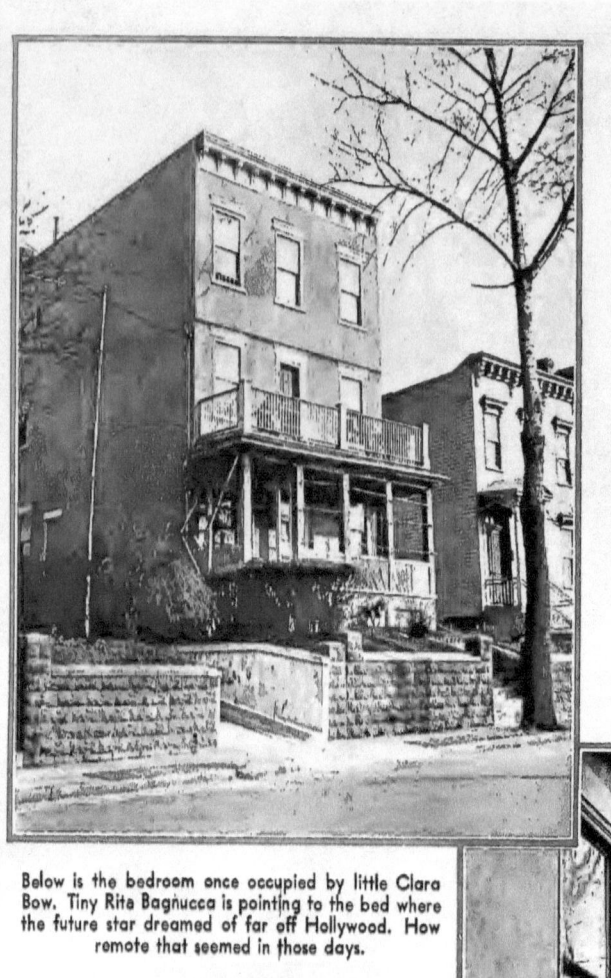

Then
and
Now

On the second floor of this unpretentious house at No. 857 73rd Street, Brooklyn, N. Y., lived the Bows in 1922. Clara Bow was then a school girl. Her father worked in Coney Island. Her mother was a bed-ridden invalid. The little red-head mailed a cheap postcard picture of herself to several motion picture magazines then conducting a contest. The winner was to be given a screen opportunity. Clara Bow won. Below is the rear entrance to the house, still owned by Mrs. Onorina Berni. Clara Bow used to sit on the second step on sunny afternoons, read of Norma Talmadge and Anita Stewart and conjure up mad fancies of stardom.

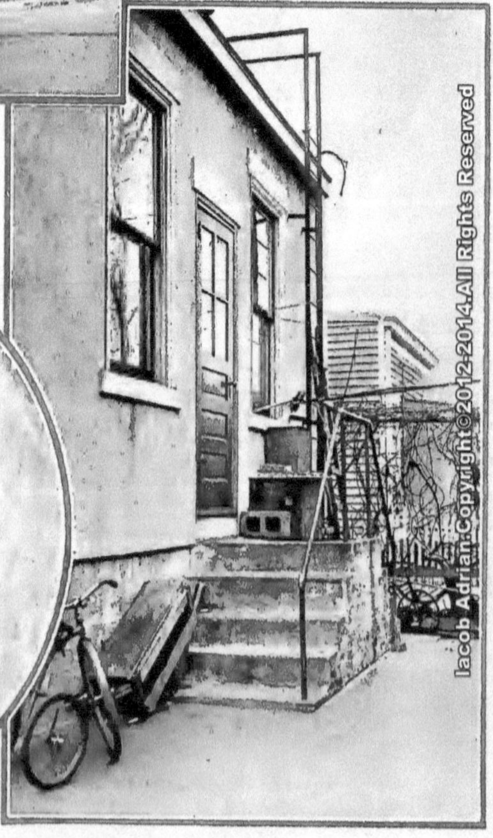

Below is the bedroom once occupied by little Clara Bow. Tiny Rita Baghucca is pointing to the bed where the future star dreamed of far off Hollywood. How remote that seemed in those days.

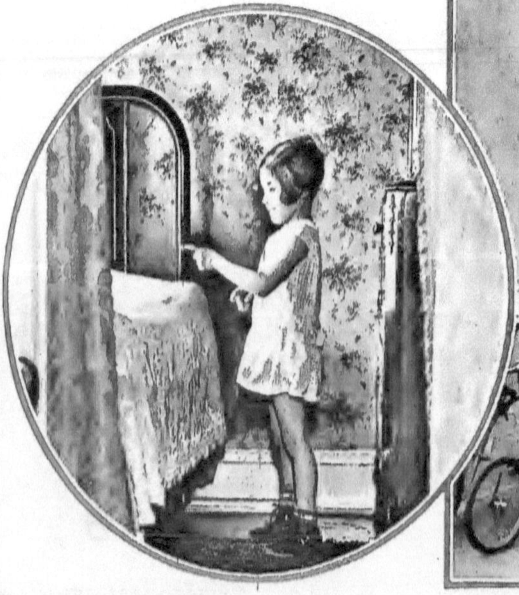

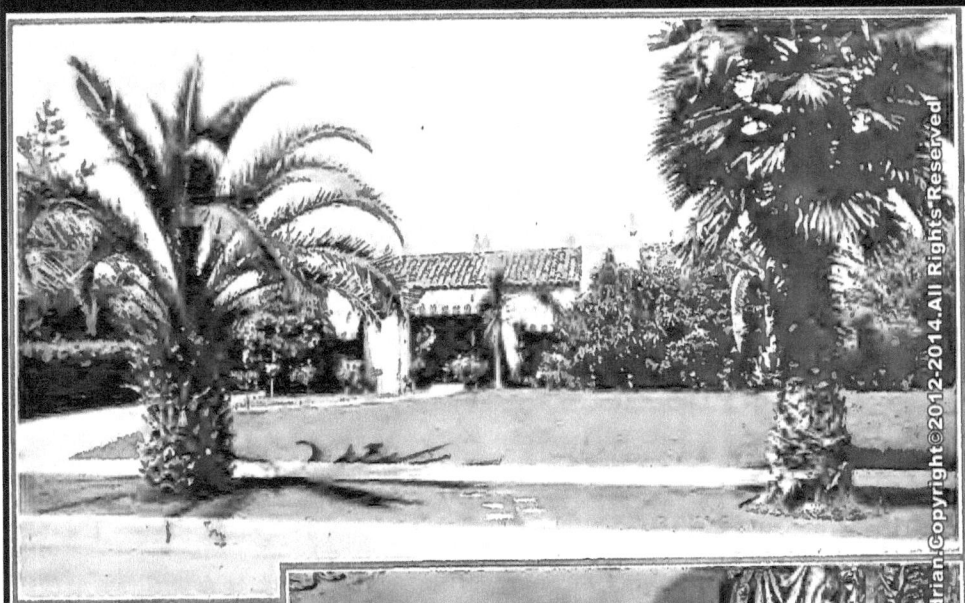

Above, the home of Clara Bow in Hollywood today. A long step from the tiny flat on 73rd Street in Brooklyn. With it has come fame and much money. Also heartaches, the pain of disillusionment and the ache of tattered romance. Little girls in quiet streets of many towns now dream of her golden fortune.

Right, the ornate bedroom of the IT girl in her Hollywood home. Here alone is Clara Bow safe from the gossip mongers bent upon tearing good fortune from her grasp. Here no doubt she herself dreams of those dingy but untroubled days in that half-forgotten Brooklyn bedroom.

Brooklyn Photographs
by Arthur Pilieri

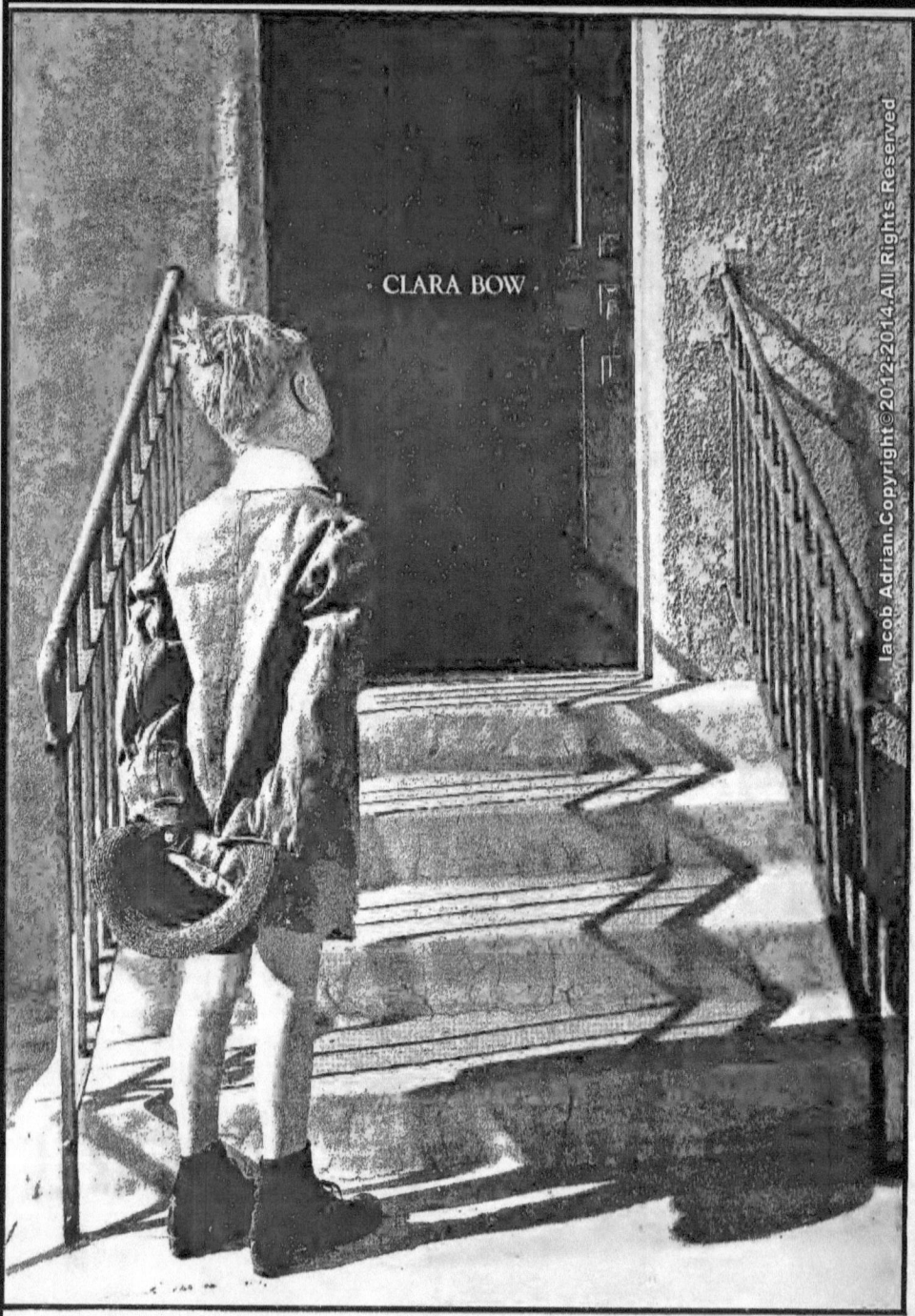

CLARA BOW

SKIPPY Skippy, Percy Crosby's lovable comic strip character, is in the movies. Skippy, in the person of young Jackie Cooper, is making a picture in Hollywood. Wait until Sooky, who is always belittlin', Cuthbert and the others of Skippy's gang hear about this. And what will Aunt Gussie and Uncle Louis the glassblower say?

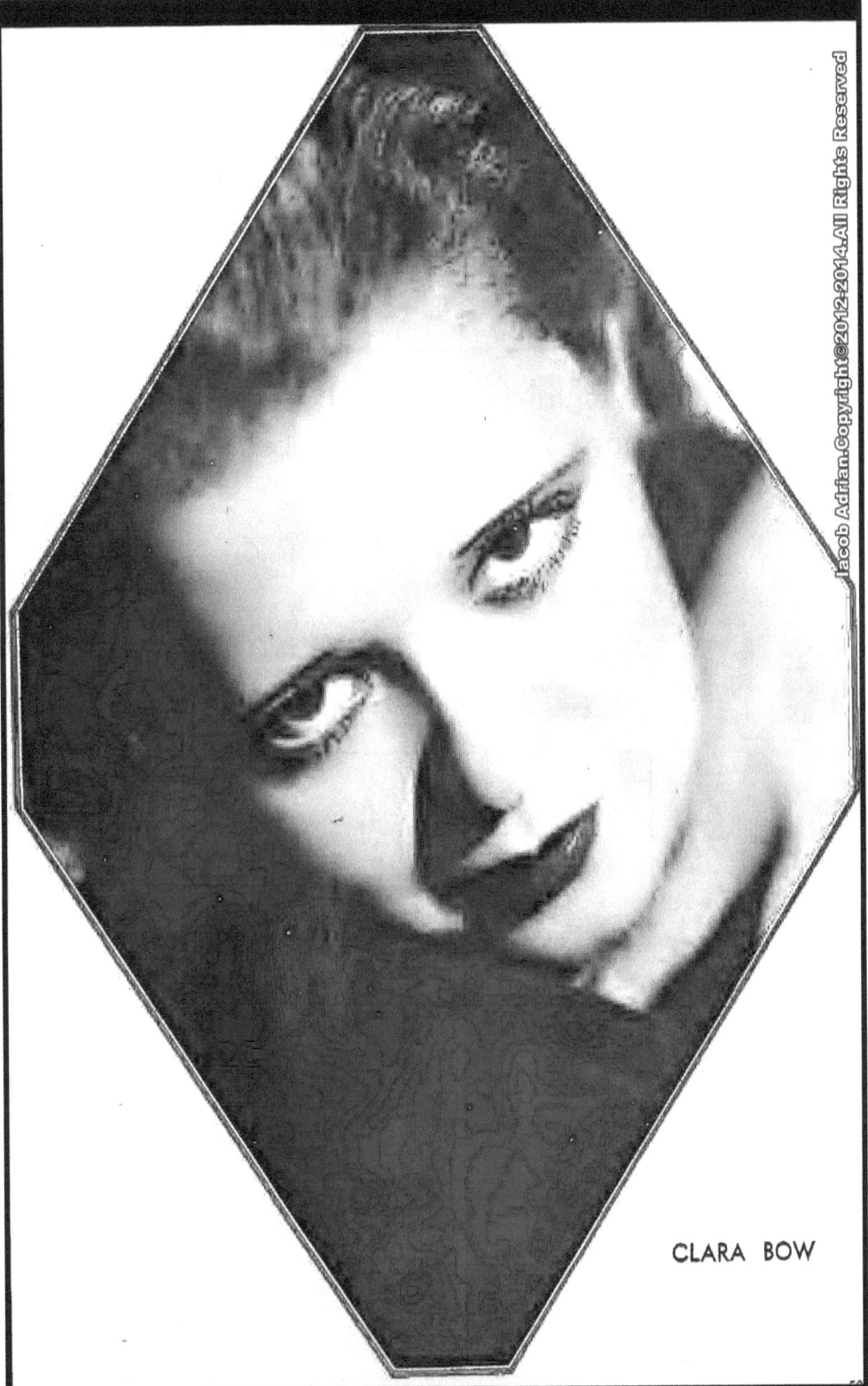

CLARA BOW

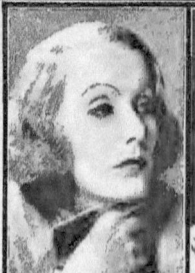
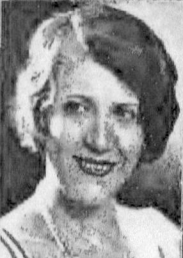
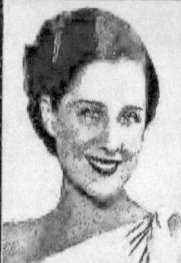
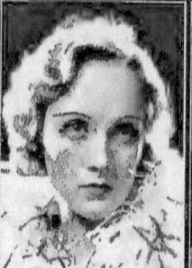
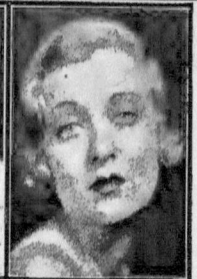

Greta Garbo
Five feet six
Weight, 125 pounds
Blue eyes, blond hair

Ruth Chatterton
Five feet two
Weight, 110 pounds
Blue eyes, brown hair

Normo Sheorer
Five feet one
Weight, 118 pounds
Blue eyes, brown hair

Morlene Dietrich
Five feet five
Weight, 120 pounds
Blue eyes, blond hair

Constance Bennett
Five feet four
Weight, 102 pounds
Blue eyes, blond hair

Here Are the Actual Figures That Will Enable You to Learn Your Screen Possibilities

FIGURING a formula for film fame! What a fancy-teasing task that is; spilling all their charms together, the pretty girls who are the screen's darlings, and the handsome interesting men. The blondes and brunettes, dark eyes and blue; the luscious curves and slender waistlines; tall, slender, interesting-looking men and burly hairy chested magnetic roughnecks! Taking them apart, bit by bit; weighing each feature and charm at the scales of the box office; then adding them all up and translating all this charm and fascination, this warm flesh and blood, this intelligence and personality, into mere terms of measurements!

It would take a cleverer person than you and I to do this gloriously impossible project as it should be done; but, at the risk of creating a lovely Frankenstein that will go to Hollywood and do untold damage, we will proceed to spill the stars into a big hopper, dismember them, and reassemble their charms by means of General Average. Then if you can add the soul to this lovely or handsome monster, perhaps success in films will be yours.

IF you have been hearing on all sides, after your striking work in the class play, that you should really go into the movies, you may take this magazine in one hand, and your mirror in the other, and in some quiet private place, determine once and for all your film possibilities. Don't forget the measuring tape and the weighing scales. And if you feel you have a camera-proof face, there's your own home

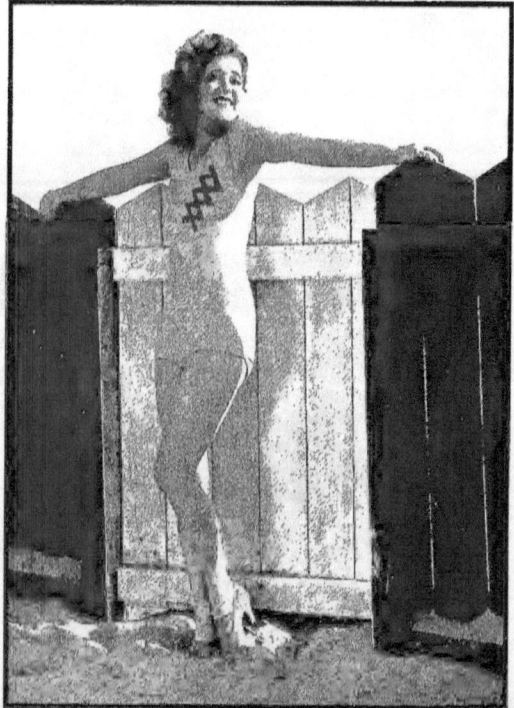

film test, as prescribed by the seven foremost casting directors in Hollywood. They are the men you would have to see and impress favorably; they are the watchdogs at that golden gate that is located in Hollywood, with waters just as rough for young sailors as the big Golden Gate at San Francisco.

In spite of the talkies, a motion-picture star must still have more than a share of good looks; it is true that some stage stars of little facial beauty have made great successes in films, but without exception these people have been possessed of great talent and have come to pictures with an established reputation from the legitimate stage. It is very doubtful if any casting director would have given Ruth Chatterton a second look, if she had come, untrained, and unsung, to Hollywood.

In all the discussions in this article, the requirements referred to are for leading men and women, who would develop into stars; character rôles, and comic rôles, are not included. The requirements for these rôles are different; but there are so many talented people available for character rôles, as compared with those available for leading rôles, that it is a field not to be considered by the young artist. Older artists of tried and trained worth more than fill these rôles.

The qualities of

With a height of five feet three and one-half inches, and a weight of 110 pounds, Clara Bow comes closest to being the perfect feminine movie star in physique, at least. Her height is exactly right and her weight fractionally so,

When LEO Rules

Leo the Lion, Having Dominion Over the Theater, Rules the Month of August, Bringing Stage and Screen Success to Many of Its Gifted Children

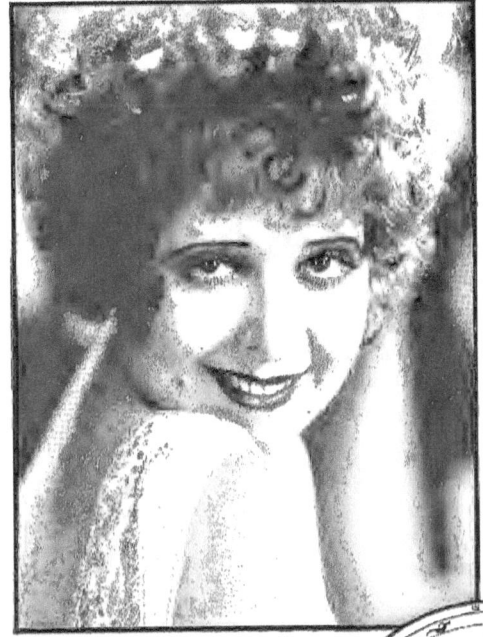

Clara Bow was born in Brooklyn at 2 A. M. on July 29, 1906. The planet Saturn was in mid-heaven. So it was with Napoleon. But Jupiter was rising. Jupiter is the planet which comes to the rescue when all seems lost. Miss Bow's future, says Evangeline Adams, depends upon herself.

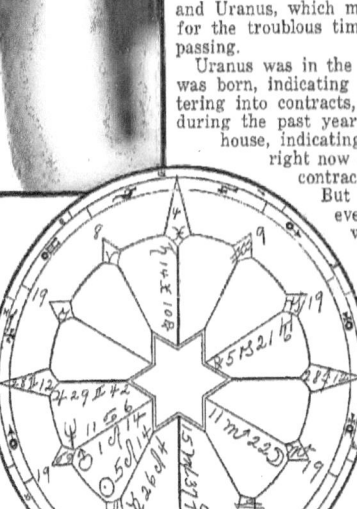

"I S Clara Bow through?"
"Can Clara come back?"

These questions are asked me more often than any others by my movie-minded clients. And now that Clara Bow's own month has come around, I am ready to give the answer of the stars.

Clara was born when the planet Saturn was in mid-heaven. So was Napoleon. So were many others, famous in history, who rose suddenly to great heights and achieved a no less sudden fall.

But Clara's fate is not so easily decided as that. If the time of her birth, as given to me, is correct, Jupiter, "the eleventh-hour friend," was rising when she was born. And Jupiter is the planet which comes to the rescue when all seems lost.

So there you have it: Saturn, who has pulled her up, is trying to pull her down; and Jupiter, always the booster, is trying to maintain her on her heights.

Jupiter is the most powerful of all the planets. But whether or not he exerts his whole strength on behalf of Clara Bow depends largely on whether Clara, herself, plays fair. Jupiter is the god of money and success; but he is also the god of honor and honorable dealing. He is a "square-shooter," this mighty Jupiter; and he helps only those who "shoot square" themselves.

I SHOULD say, then, that the answer to the first question, "Is she through?" is "Not necessarily"; and the answer to the second question, "Can she come back?" is "Yes—if she behaves herself."

Recently, Clara's stars have been nothing to brag about. She has been suffering for about two years from an affliction of the two sinister planets Saturn and Uranus, which more than accounts astrologically for the troublous times through which she has been passing.

Uranus was in the house of partnerships when she was born, indicating that she should be wary of entering into contracts, matrimonial or otherwise; and during the past year, Saturn, too, has been in that house, indicating that she is in especial danger right now of breaking her present business contract or having it broken for her.

But the chances of Clara surviving even that blow are better than they would be with most people. The Moon, which governs her relations with the public, and has been of great use to her in gathering her large following, was in the house of pleasure and the theater when she was born. It is unlikely, with such a Moon—friendly to Neptune, Saturn and Uranus —that this young lady will ever be obscure.

Incidentally, Miss Bow has the Sun and Mars in conjunction, which invariably shows danger of trouble with men. And she has Saturn and Uranus unfriendly to Jupiter, a combination which indicates loss of money by theft!

After Clara Bow's storm chart, Norma Shearer's seems like a sunlit sea. Miss Shearer was also born strongly under the influence of Leo, the Lion; but since Neptune was rising in the sign Gemini at the moment of her birth—according to the hour that has been given me—it was inevitable that she should work out her career on a somewhat more intellectual plane. Moreover, she has the Moon in Aquarius, which makes her, astrologically as well as dramatically, always the lady. Her instinct is ever to do the right thing, and, if possible, the fine and helpful thing.

THE reasons for her success, according to astrology, are obvious. Mars, the planet which gives initiative, industry and ambition, was very powerfully placed when Miss Shearer was born. Neptune, the planet ruling her chosen profession, is the dominant planet in her horoscope, her star of destiny. The Moon, ruling

the Heavens

BY EVANGELINE ADAMS

her relations with the public, was in the mid-heaven when she was born, which always brings publicity, and often fame. And Jupiter, ruling honor, glory, money and success, was in its own sign, Sagittarius, and friendly to Mercury, the God of the Mind.

These facts should answer once for all a question which is often asked about Miss Shearer. You hear it sometimes in the audiences, even at her best pictures. "Oh, yes, she's a good actress, all right, but would she be where she is today if she hadn't married Irving Thalberg?" The answer to that is "Unequivocally yes!" In fact, there is nothing in Miss Shearer's horoscope which indicates that any marriage she might have made would have been especially lucky for her in a professional way. On the other hand, there is every indication that her greatest happiness as well as her greatest success will always depend on her sticking to her work and standing absolutely on her own feet.

As for Miss Shearer's immediate future, there can be little doubt of its success, for she is coming under the best astrological conditions that she has been under for many years. Let's hope that she makes the most of them!

A GOOD many prominent stage folk, including the late David Belasco, William Gillette and George Bernard Shaw, were born in this period governed by Leo; so were Ethel Barrymore, Julia Marlowe, Pauline Lord, Elsie Ferguson and Alla Nazimova. Of course, there's a reason for this. But I have been so interested in Miss Bow and Miss Shearer that I have forgotten to tell you what it is. We found that April was a big month for movie stars because Aries, the sign of the Zodiac which presides over a good part of that month, is the sign of leadership; Aries people get to the top. May was a good month, too; a great many artists who have achieved special prominence since the coming of the talking pictures were born during this month; and the astrological reason, as you may remember, was that Taurus is the sign of the Zodiac which rules the throat. Now we have August, with its host of successful stars; and the reason is again astrologically inevitable. Leo the Lion, the sign which rules the last days of July and the first twenty-three days of August, governs the house of pleasure in the astrological heavens, and in that capacity has dominion over the theater.

Two of the stage stars in the list I just gave have tried their art with considerable success in the movies, and their stars indicate that they may "come back" at a not too distant date to achieve new triumphs. I refer to those beautiful daughters of Leo, Elsie Ferguson and Alla Nazimova.

Miss Ferguson, for example, is under more favorable aspects *right* now for her work than she has been for many moons; and in 1932, the heavens will seem to *conspire* to do her honor. Jupiter will be in Miss Ferguson's own sign, and will be favorable to *four* of her most important planets. If she takes advantage of these favoring influences and does not allow personal matters to interfere with her art she may achieve heights of which she has never before dreamed.

But the most interesting thing about Miss Ferguson's

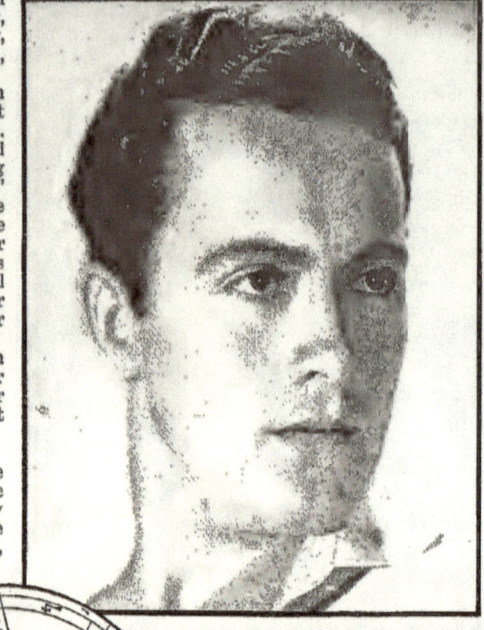

The relation of Venus to Neptune in Buddy Rogers' chart is similar to that in Rudolph Valentino's, says Miss Adams. It gives him the power to play the lover. The planets indicate luck in the arts. The position of both Venus and Neptune intimates that his voice may yet be his fortune.

horoscope is not the good aspects under which she is coming, but the amazingly bad ones through which she has just been struggling. To many of her admirers it may seem strange that this beautiful and popular actress has fallen so far short of the success that should be hers during these last three years, but it isn't at all strange to an astrologer. Uranus and Neptune, the actors' planets, have been unfriendly to her Moon, ruling the *public*: to her Jupiter, ruling *finances;* to her Venus, ruling her *art;* and to her Mercury, ruling her *state of mind.* Under such conditions it was next to impossible for her to find a suitable play or to succeed in it if she did find it.

IN Nazimova's case the reason for her "up-and-down-and-up" career is astrologically obvious. She has Venus in Cancer, the Moon's own sign, and inasmuch as the Moon rules the public she was destined to deal with people in the mass. Her Venus is also friendly to Mars, bringing the two sex signs together and giving her power and passion in her art. And her Jupiter is favorable to Neptune, indicating the success and glory she was to achieve in her work, but—since Neptune is uncertain as well as

When Leo Rules the Heavens

inspirational—also indicating the period of great reverses which have characterized her meteoric career. I am very glad that she is now coming more strongly under both Venus and her own sign Leo than she has been for a long time. If she takes full advantage of these favoring planetary conditions, she may not only continue to display the superb talents which she has been exercising in recent years in behalf of Miss Le Gallienne's repertory company and the Theater Guild, but she may once more scale the heights of financial success and great popular acclaim on the screen.

Pauline Frederick is another gifted daughter of Leo who is coming under better planetary influences for her work than she has been under for some years. In fact, almost everybody born at about this time — whether they are in the movies or not —will be very strongly under the influence of the beneficent planet Jupiter through the Fall of 1931 and the Spring and Summer of 1932! The list of movie notables who will be so favored, unless their individual horoscopes are grievously afflicted, includes: Cecil and William de Mille, Lawrence Gray, William Powell, Helen Kane, Rudy Vallee, Colleen Moore, Sylvia Sidney, Charles Farrell, Dorothy Jordan, Anita Page, Eleanor Boardman, and—perhaps, most interesting of all —Buddy Rogers. Mr. Rogers

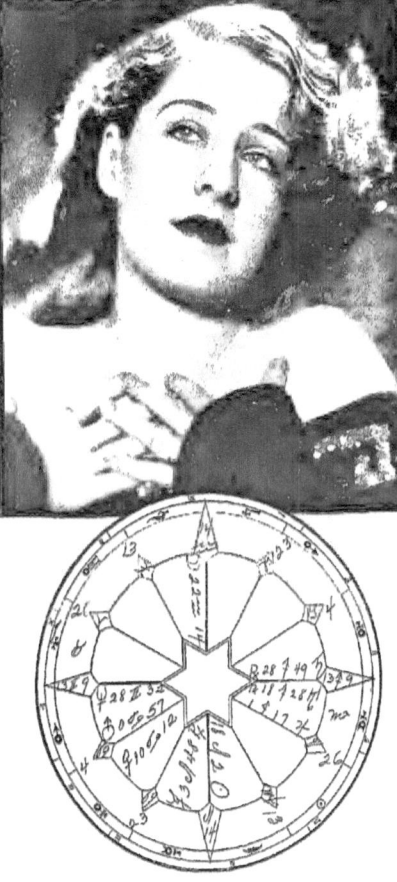

Norma Shearer's astrological chart is like a sunlit sea in comparison with Clara Bow's stormy one. The reasons for her success are obvious. Mars, giving initiative, industry and ambition, was very powerfully placed when she was born.

will feel the Jupiter influence —but with variations!

MR. ROGERS' Moon, ruling his relations with the public, is in Virgo; also his Mercury, the planet which rules the intellect. And inasmuch as Virgo is itself a highly intellectual sign, there is every reason why this young man, at a very early age, has proved so intelligent and thorough in the interpretation of his parts. Buddy's Venus—and, believe me, Venus is a very important planet in the horoscope of a movie actor!—is in favorable aspect to Jupiter, which makes him lucky in his arts, and to Neptune, which gives him the power of visualization.

This relation of Venus to Neptune in Mr. Rogers' chart is similar to the one in Rudolph Valentino's. It gives him the power to play the lover on the screen in such a convincing way—although we all know that he doesn't feel it at the time—that we can't help falling in love with him, or rather with his

---

IF YOUR BIRTHDAY COMES IN AUGUST

IF you were born between July 24th and August 28rd, you belong to the noble sign Leo, symbolized by the Lion and ruled by the Sun.

If you are a typical son or daughter of Leo, you are the masterful, high-minded type, possessing great executive ability. You may exercise this ability in either business or social life. Leo is the royal sign. Leo people are kings of the circle to which they belong.

Leo people are generous, even to the point of extravagance. They have magnetic personalities. They should always see in person those whom they wish to influence. They also have a natural dislike for anything petty or underhanded. They are ambitious, industrious,

untiring, but they dislike menial tasks. They should not let their ambition make them unhappy.

One trouble with Leo people is that they want to rule in *everything*. They should not try to be the dominating force all the time. Their magnetic personalities and inherent abilities will attract the big things to them, anyway. They should let other people have their way in the non-essentials. Their energies are too valuable to dissipate.

Another danger which Leo people face is the temptation to "show off." Leo people are good, and they know it. So does everybody else. They don't need to impress others with their ability. It sticks out all over them. And

they should be sparing also with their authority. He who has the greatest authority seldom shows it.

Leo rules the heart. All people born strongly under its influence should look out for all kinds of heart trouble; also for strains and other accidents to the back.

The natives of this sign are natural executives. If they can't be at the head of the business in which they are engaged—and not everybody can—they should be connected if possible with the executive branch.

Leo people are apt to find their most congenial life partners among those who are born strongly under the influence of Sagittarius or Aries.

When Leo Rules the Heavens

shadow. His Moon, which governs his relations with older women, is in aspect to Uranus, which gives him unusual powers over older and married women. That is great for his screen career, but it may cause him some trouble in real life!

His Sun is also friendly to Uranus, which usually indicates a fine background—and I understand the position of Mr. Rogers' family in the community and his own education are somewhat more advanced than is often the case with our popular favorites. This fact has been a great asset to him in the type of parts he depicts as has his voice. The position of both Venus and Neptune in his horoscope indicates that he could have developed a very fine singing voice. In fact, his voice may yet be his fortune.

But enough of Mr. Rogers, and Miss Shearer, and Miss Bow and all the rest!

We mustn't let these shining personalities obscure the fact that *everybody* born between July 24th and August 23rd belongs to this royal sign Leo and that *every* Leo person in greater or lesser degree is coming under most auspicious conditions beginning with the Fall of 1931 and extending through 1932.

This applies to these lions and lionesses we have been discussing this month. It applies also, if you are a true son or daughter of Leo, to *you!*

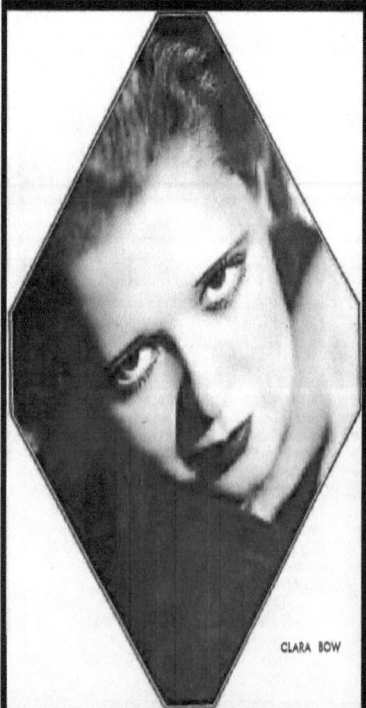

CLARA BOW

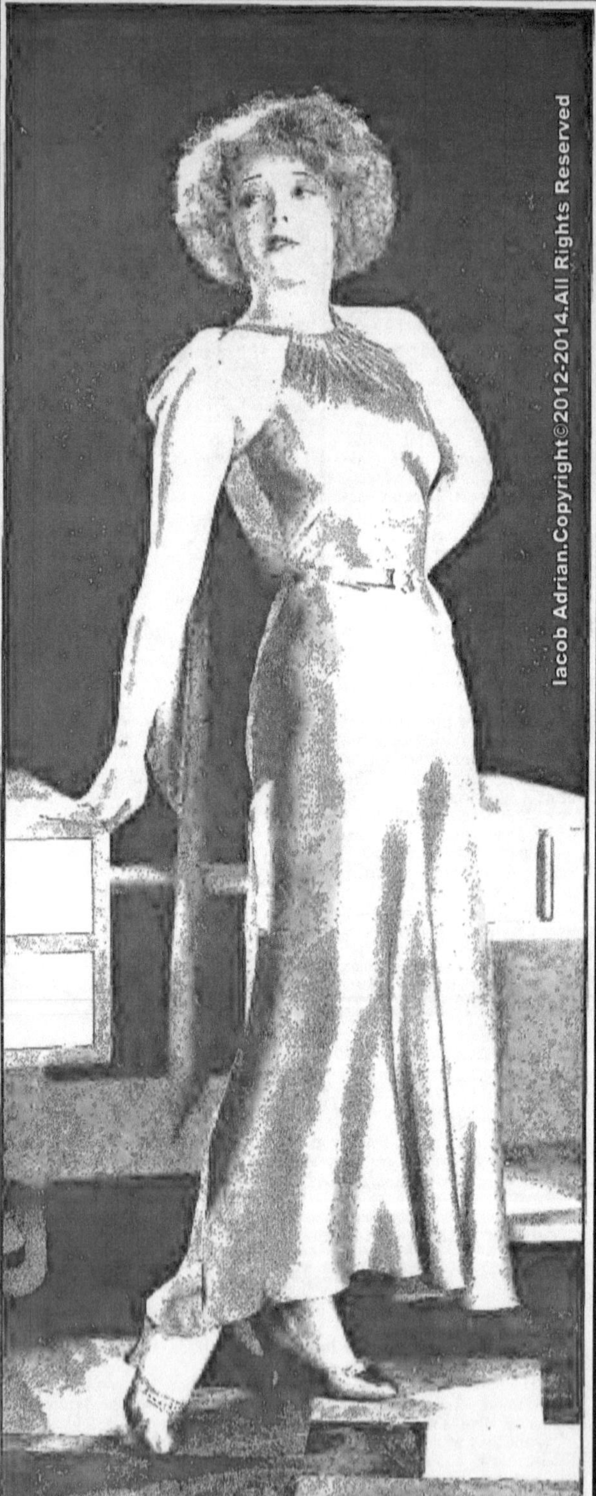

Gossip of the Studios

"I am one of those people that carry a camera, a good one, too, along wherever they go and never take a picture. You have known such fools before, else I should send the magazine a snapshot of myself. Can't do that but I do ask you to put a line in to stop the rumors popping up again about my having a relapse. Don't know how such rumors get about. Perhaps because I've stayed over here so long. At any rate they are not true. I am feeling grand—having a peach of a time enjoying myself. Between visits home here with Mother and Father I've managed to get about a bit. Made two visits to Stockholm, been to Berlin, two weeks in Vienna, four weeks in Nice, Cannes and Antibes, back to Sweden again where I will spend the rest of the time with the folks and paying visits to relatives before sailing in July. Going the long way round, through Panama Canal. I won't be back in California till August—back and ready to try my luck in the talkies if the Powers That Be give me a look-in. Hope you can read this very bad scribble. The pen is worn out and so is my hand. Have had one of them there letter-writing spells today."

JACKIE COOPER is proud of the watch he received as a gift from Percy Crosby, creator of "Skippy," but wishes it were a nickel-plated affair instead of the solid gold kind. "It's so good I have to keep it in a vault," wailed Jackie.

Madge Evans, erstwhile child star, now a grown-up leading lady for Metro-Goldwyn-Mayer, admitted she one time posed for a brewery advertisement. "But it was good beer!" she exclaimed.

THE secret of Bayard Veiller's preference for writing for the talking screen over the theater at last is out.

The master of mystery thrillers was discussing "Guilty Hands," his new murder story in which Lionel Barrymore is featured.

"A talkie only requires one-fourth of the dialogue needed for a stage play," he said. "On the stage the plot is unfolded three-quarters by words. On the screen it is three-quarters visual and one-quarter words, thank goodness!"

EDNA MARION, Wampus baby Star of a few years ago, is now in the costume jewelry business, with a shop on Hollywood Boulevard.

NO rocking chair old-age is going to have a chance to catch up with Marie Dressler.

Just last year Marie dashed to Europe for what she called a rest. Then she traipsed over to Hawaii for another "rest," but found the social whirl too taxing. Now, on completing "Emma," she is off again for Europe to visit friends in England and Germany.

"And I'm not going to Bad-Norheim!" she announces.

LOOKS like Joan Crawford will just have to have a baby to satisfy Hollywood rumors.

Ever since she married Doug Jr., Joan has been reported "expecting". But it isn't true. At least Joan says so, and she ought to know!

CHARLES STARRETT, Billie Dove's new leading man, is the chap who escaped death by a contract.

He was scheduled to go to Labrador with Varick Frissell who made "The Viking," for retakes. He had the leading rôle in the picture but couldn't return because he'd signed a contract with Paramount.

The ship was blown up on the return trip and Frissell and many others perished.

JOHN WRAY, whose biggest claim to screen fame was as "Himmelstoss" in "All Quiet," admits to learning his rôle in "Silence" by sleeping on the script for several nights.

It's an old stage superstition that must make for uncomfortable sleeping. You wake up with lines on your back and in your head.

Dorothy Burgess, who makes her living playing señoritas with trick accents, (witness "In Old Arizona" and "Lasca of the Rio Grande"), cannot speak Spanish.

TRAGEDY stalked in Hollywood when Evalyn Knapp fell down a 30-foot embankment and fractured her spine.

Miss Knapp was just getting ahead at First National—had a big rôle in "Smart Money" and "The Millionaire."

She will be laid up for six months before she faces a camera again.

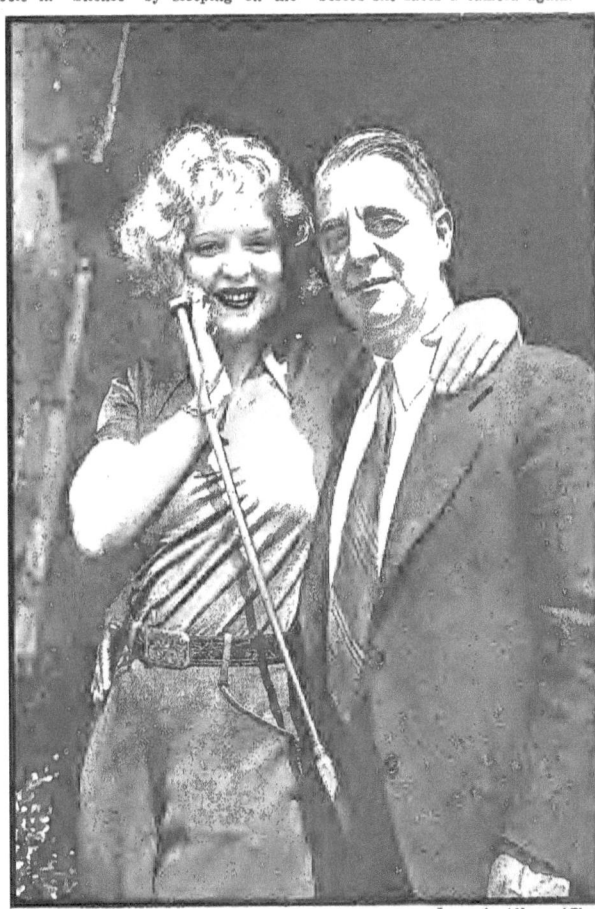

Clara Bow is spending two months resting at a ranch in Nevada. During that time she will consider just what next to do. She has a release from her Paramount contract and she may sign with another producing concern. Or she may try vaudeville. Anyway, she is going to spend her spare time writing the real story of her life. Miss Bow, who is shown above with her father, is no longer a red head. She is a blonde, as you can see.

The Hollywood Racket of Making Movie Stars Into Something They Are Not Goes Merrily On

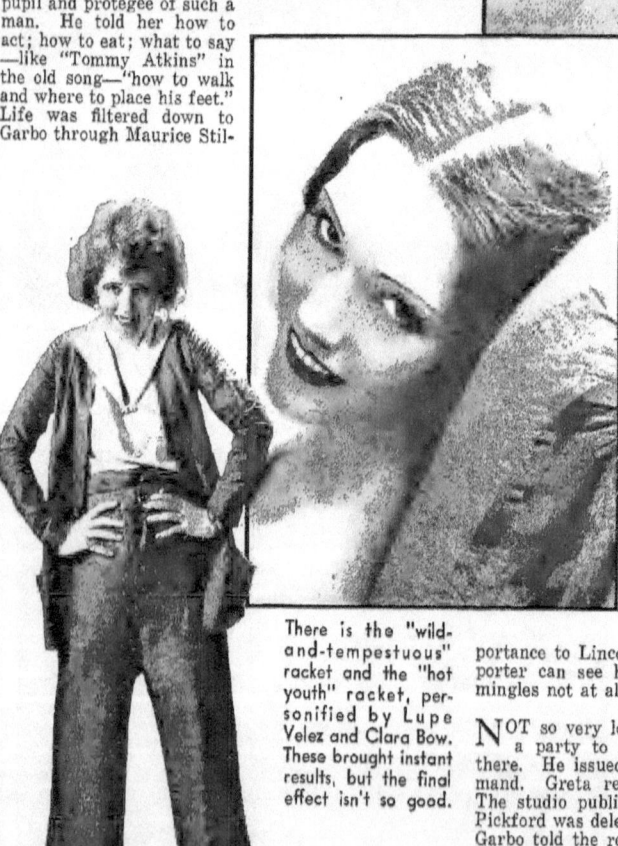

steamboat. So it was left to years and to others to work this gag up to the Garbo point of efficiency.

The truth about Garbo is that—like Lillian Gish—she is very timid and frightened. And there is also another compelling reason.

Greta was brought to the United States by Stiller, the great Swedish director. He was more than just a director. He was a near diety in Europe. When a print of a Stiller picture came out, all the other studios grabbed it. The other great directors stopped work and rushed to the projection rooms—with stenographers. They took down breathless bulletins—"he showed a close in silhouette," "he panned down from the sixth story over the front of the hotel," etc., etc.

You can imagine what it meant to Garbo to be the pupil and protégée of such a man. He told her how to act; how to eat; what to say —like "Tommy Atkins" in the old song—"how to walk and where to place his feet." Life was filtered down to Garbo through Maurice Stil-

The best-dressed-woman-in-Hollywood racket has been worked by many stars of stage and screen. But no one ever brought it to the state of perfection won by Gloria Swanson. Miss Swanson hates to dress up for the films—but it is the only sure way to success.

There is the "wild-and-tempestuous" racket and the "hot youth" racket, personified by Lupe Velez and Clara Bow. These brought instant results, but the final effect isn't so good.

ler. In the United States, a movie miracle happened. Stiller, the great director, flopped; Garbo, the little protégée and pupil, became a great star. He died of a broken heart. Without him Garbo was not sure what to do. She was a ship without a rudder. As a cautious Swede, she solved the problem by keeping out of sight and saying nothing.

She probably knows what to say now, but keeps up the act for two reasons. It is a good commercial gag and if she started in to talk now—after so much thought and studied silence—she would have to say something at least equal in importance to Lincoln's speech at Gettysburg. So no reporter can see her; she will not go to parties; she mingles not at all.

NOT so very long ago a great publisher was giving a party to some Big Shots. He wanted Garbo there. He issued an invitation that was a royal command. Greta refused. She said she was too tired. The studio publicity men pleaded to no avail. Mary Pickford was delegated to herd her in. No go. At last Garbo told the real truth. To a last appeal she whispered pathetically, "I can't go. I'm afraid."

To one party of girls she was inveigled. She came in boys' shoes and a boy's coat. Nobody saw her after she got there. The hostess found her at last sitting on the fence of the horse corral looking at the sunset. "Oh," she gasped in ecstasy. "I tell you what I love. I love to smell horses and look at sunsets."

The monastic seclusion of Ramon Novarro was built on the same pattern. Herb

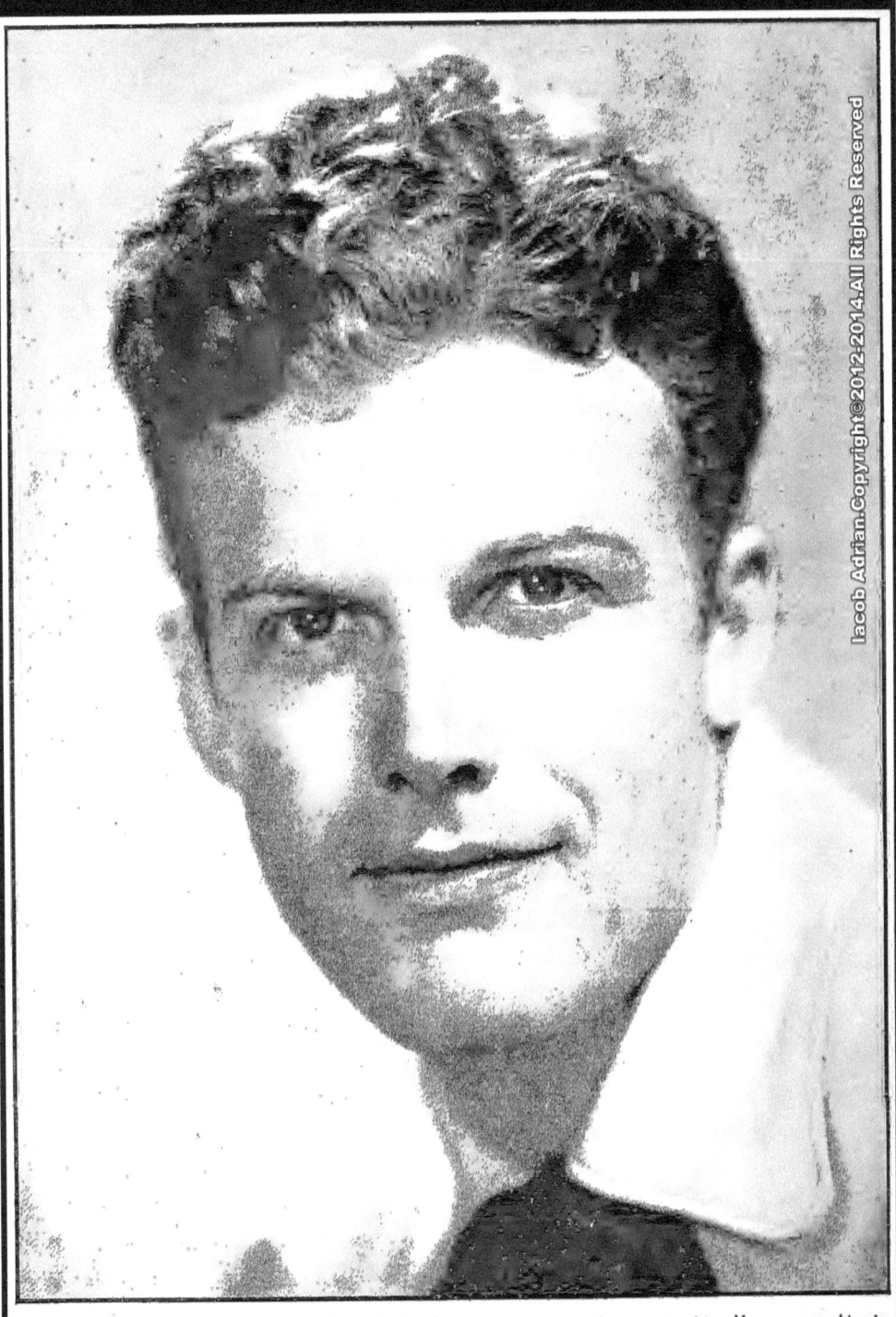

CLARA BOW'S BOY FRIEND—REX BELL. Also her business manager and severest critic. You can see him in Universal's "Battling With Buffalo Bill" if you want to. Bell was born in Chicago in 1906 and migrated to Hollywood with his parents when he was a small boy. Attended Hollywood High School. Started in motion pictures with Buck Jones and later played with Tom Mix. Those two stars gave him an all round training in the old fashioned school of Western melodrama. Everybody who knows Bell says he is a swell chap. And so does Clara Bow.

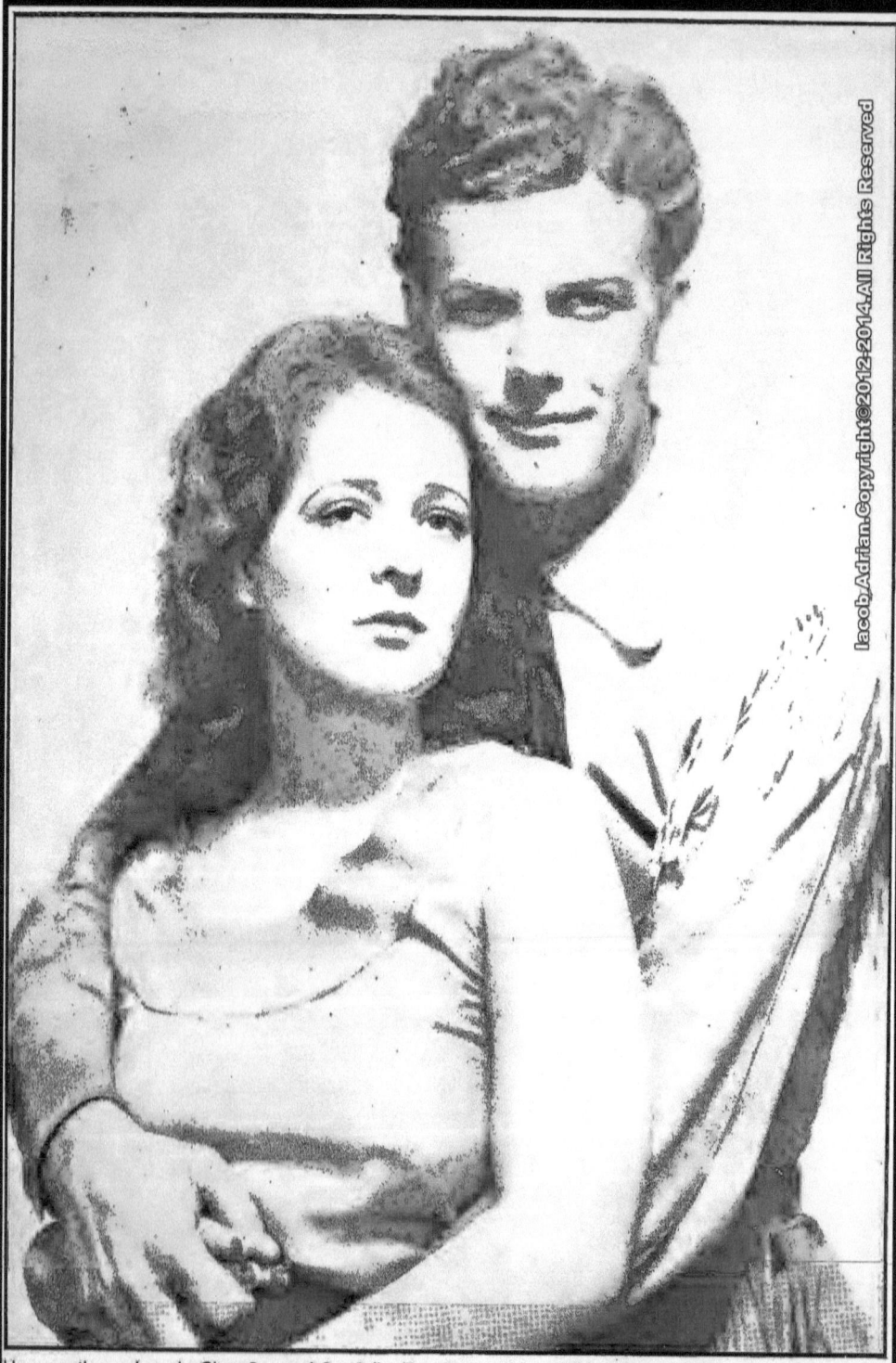

Here are the newly-weds, Clara Bow and Rex Bell. They became Mr. and Mrs. George F. Belham at a late evening ceremony performed at Las Vegas, Nevada, in December. After the honeymoon Clara will finish a feature talkie for Columbia Pictures. At last reports Rex was still denying the marriage.

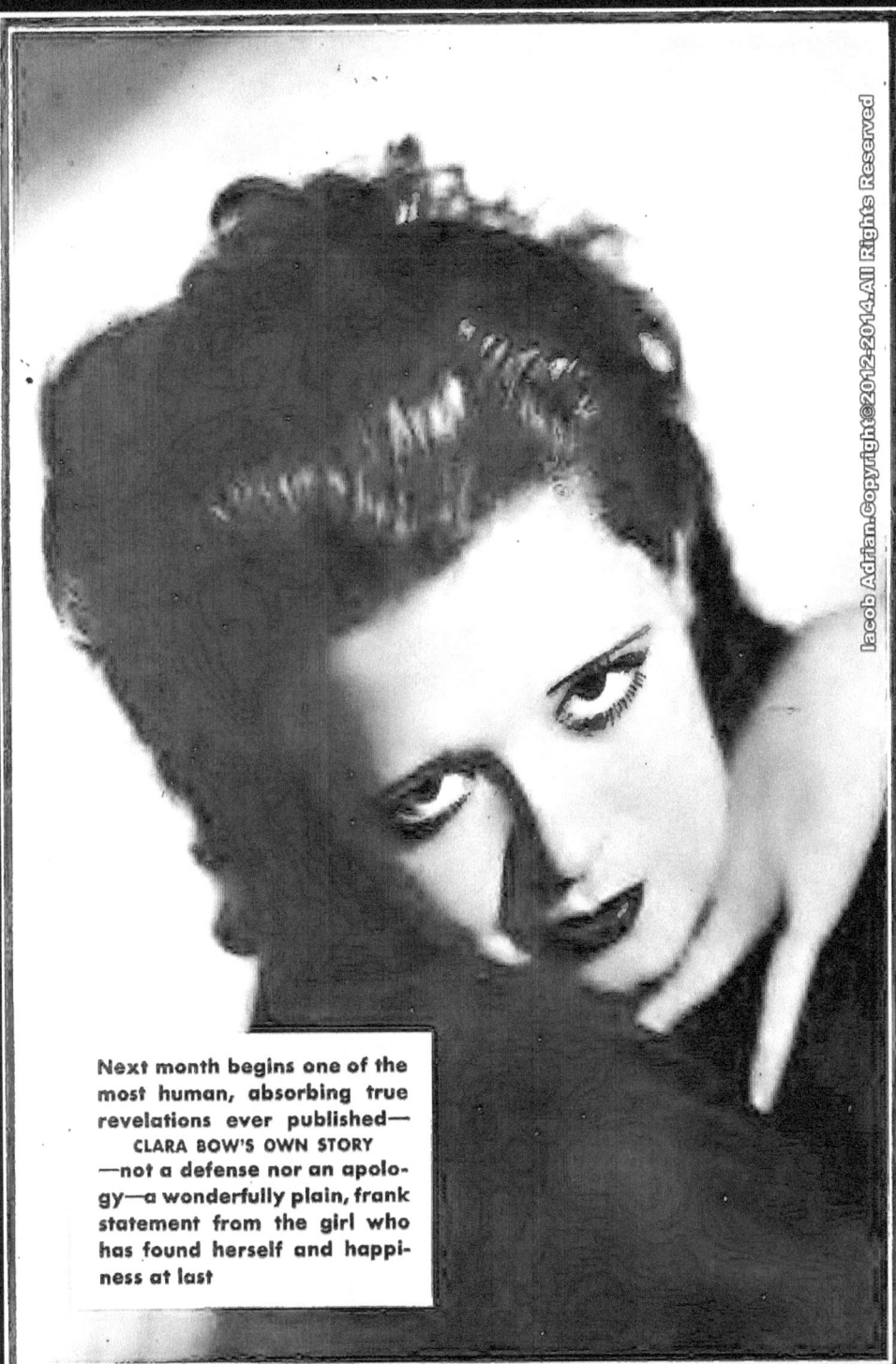

Next month begins one of the most human, absorbing true revelations ever published— CLARA BOW'S OWN STORY —not a defense nor an apology—a wonderfully plain, frank statement from the girl who has found herself and happiness at last

CLARA BOW

Announcement: ELSIE JANIS, noted star, joins The New Movie staff, turning the spotlight on her friend, CLARA BOW—

THERE, Little Girl, DON'T CRY

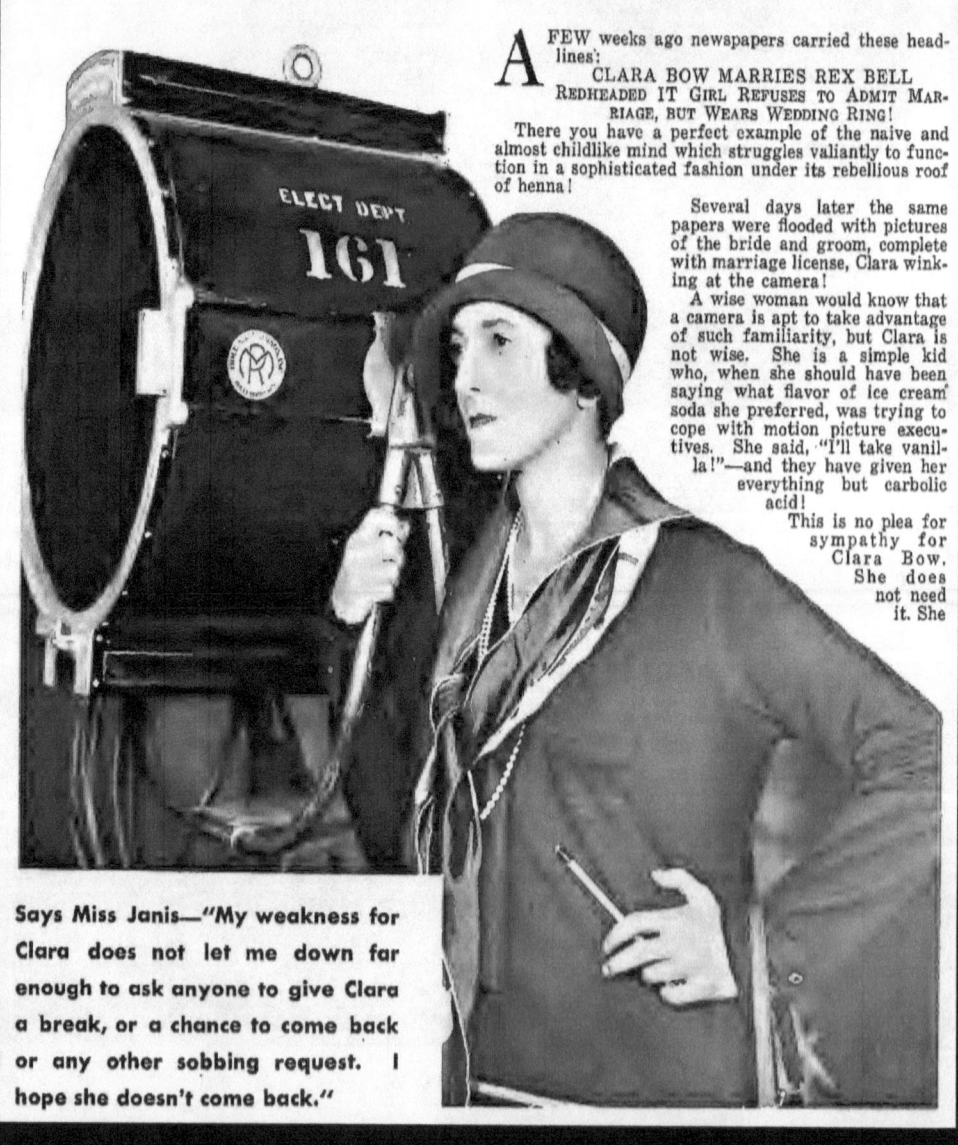

A FEW weeks ago newspapers carried these headlines:

CLARA BOW MARRIES REX BELL
REDHEADED IT GIRL REFUSES TO ADMIT MARRIAGE, BUT WEARS WEDDING RING!

There you have a perfect example of the naive and almost childlike mind which struggles valiantly to function in a sophisticated fashion under its rebellious roof of henna!

Several days later the same papers were flooded with pictures of the bride and groom, complete with marriage license, Clara winking at the camera!

A wise woman would know that a camera is apt to take advantage of such familiarity, but Clara is not wise. She is a simple kid who, when she should have been saying what flavor of ice cream soda she preferred, was trying to cope with motion picture executives. She said, "I'll take vanilla!"—and they have given her everything but carbolic acid!

This is no plea for sympathy for Clara Bow. She does not need it. She

Says Miss Janis—"My weakness for Clara does not let me down far enough to ask anyone to give Clara a break, or a chance to come back or any other sobbing request. I hope she doesn't come back."

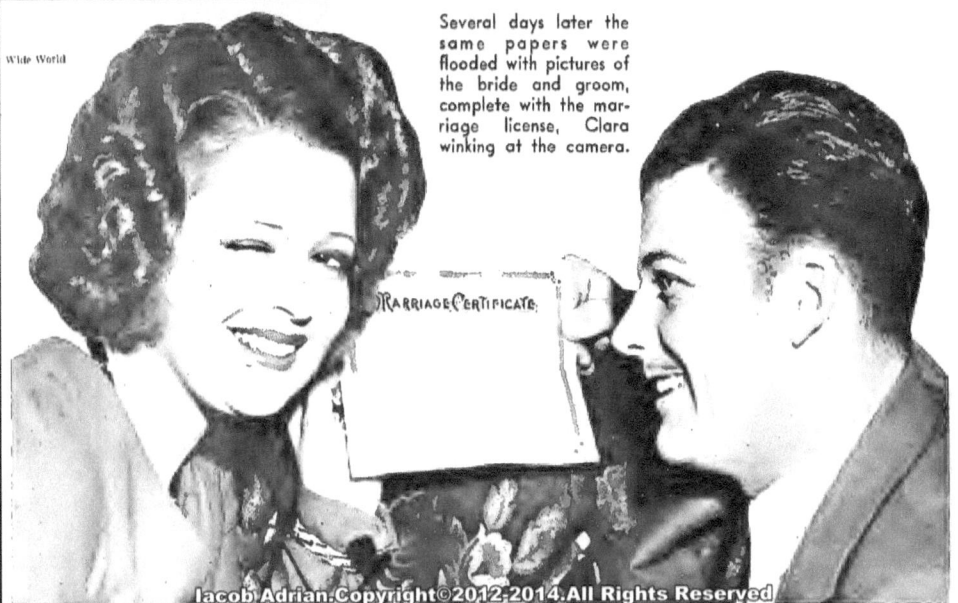

Several days later the same papers were flooded with pictures of the bride and groom, complete with the marriage license, Clara winking at the camera.

Wide World

is a great person, a great actress if given the right opportunity, and a great friend if given the right understanding! Now, after trying all sorts of stimulants, sedatives and fiancés, she has found an antidote—Clara has "rung the Bell" and its tone is one of purity and unselfishness.

Many men have loved Clara Bow, the Paradox of Paramount, but Rex Bell has married "a baby from Brooklyn," who lost her illusions in an avalanche of close-ups and has been looking for them ever since.

MY personal experience with the Blind Bow Girl (apologies to Carl Van Vechten) was illuminating and stimulating.

I had thoroughly resented her publicity and didn't care whether she had "It," that, and those, with a *quelque chose* thrown in. Being one who had really worked for my billing from the ripe old age of five, I disapproved of any one who could soar from a popularity contest in Brooklyn to a top spot in the Hollywood constellation on the wings of "It"!

Then I met her. Despite all the misdirected press-agent bunk about Clara's being the sizzling hot-shot of the screen, the truth is that she has a very definite flame, but it must be carefully fanned. Too strong a breeze, it flares and burns itself out, leaving nothing but the cold ashes of public criticism; too weak, and it dies in the depths of her heavily lashed eyes.

The steady fuel of friendship is what she needs. It is what she has found in Rex Bell and in a small way I think that is what she sensed in my feeling toward her.

When I arrived on the set at the studio in Hollywood to try and convince her that she should appear in the revue, "Paramount on Parade," which I was supervising, and in which every luminary under the Paramount banner had agreed to take part, with the exception of Clara, I was informed that Miss Bow did not like any one to watch her in her scenes.

I thought, "Well, really!—and this from Brooklyn."

I sneaked around and found a spot where I could watch without being caught, fully expecting to see a somewhat arrogant and headstrong upstart, refusing to take direction, no doubt.

I saw a discouraged

child looking at the microphone as if it had been Big Bertha or any other long-range gun. I heard her falter in her lines and look at the director with an expression that would wring sympathy from an income-tax collector.

"I'm terrible!" she said as she forgot her lines and the director called "Cut!"

I wanted to cry out, "You're wonderful, because you know you're terrible."

I had been on many sets where the sound equipment of the talkies was hitching its wagon to a star whose silence had been golden. I had seen them not only forget their lines but their location and the fact that the microphone picks up bad language with the same facility with which it swallows bad dialogue.

I had never heard anyone admit that she was terrible, and I had never seen anyone whom I wanted so much to put my arms about and whisper to "There, little girl, don't cry!"

I got no chance to follow my inclination, however, for Clara had been forewarned that it was my job to convince every star on the lot that their scene would be the best one in the revue. When, during a short wait, I was introduced to her, she eyed me so coldly that I talked about the weather, murmured, "James, my sables!" and left.

"Perhaps we can get along without Bow after all," I said when I got back to the front office, still shivering from my encounter with the Ball of Fire. But to myself I said confidentially, "She has simply lost her faith in Santa Claus. I'll go without my beard next time."

MEANWHILE I entered the office each day, saying, "Good morning; what about Bow?"

"Forget about her; she won't come in," I was told.

"Perhaps she won't," I said, "but I can't forget about her." And I didn't.

Months passed. I saw her occasionally in the studio restaurant. The revue was nearing completion and Clara was nearing a breakdown. Her love affairs were being dragged through the streets of Hollywood like the football pennants of the losing side. I had written a song for her, called "There Ought to Be More Like You," but

Next Month Clara Bow Gives Advice to

Girls Who Aspire to Become Movie Stars

Leap Year Valentine

JOHN GILBERT: A used husband, but promises well. Likes to talk big words such as "colossal." To get on his good side, give him unabridged dictionary. Lost fortune on Wall Street and yearns to get it back from Wall Street; therefore, his wife may anticipate being financially ruined any old day.

RUSSELL GLEASON: Young, undeveloped, but promising. Wants to be business man and usually loses money in such ventures. Likes to take weekend trips, dresses for dinner and hates onions, so cut them off your menu or you'll lose Russell. Overgrown kid and does such things as riding bicycle full tilt into ballroom. Dances well and likes it. The girl Russell marries must be a good dancer—or else.

WILLIAM HAINES: Likes women older than himself. Enjoys playing jokes and wife must learn to enjoy them—at her own expense. Gives big parties. Likes antiques (not referring to his women companions). Clever bridge player and dislikes unclever partners.

JAMES HALL: In middle thirties, average height, cheerful. A cinch for any pretty girl. Loans money without provocation. Very careless about spending. Will buy anything a good salesman wants to sell him.

JOHN HOLLAND: Tall, has blue-gray eyes and black hair. Inherited money and need not work. Plays poor game of golf, nearly always alone.

MATTY KEMP: Having tough time. Must marry money; others not wanted. Fickle; has never gone long with one girl. Has done little picture work and threatens to quit for another business, such as stock broker or bond salesman. Inclined to gain weight around the middle. Good fellow among men and inclined to be late for dates. His wife will wait for him on street corners.

ALEXANDER KIRKLAND: Earning good salary with Fox. Paints on canvas, using pretty girls for models—oh! or! Vagabond by nature, and goes off on unexpected hikes. His wife must get used to this wanderlust and accustom herself to living without him for days at a time—ahem, perhaps convenient.

ERIC LINDEN: Very young and deludes himself he is sophisticated. Fickle. If you marry Eric, your struggles will commence; you'll have to hold him. Admits he is a genius and excuses his own temperamental outbreaks with the admission. Has bright prospects. Any woman marrying Eric now and mastering him may raise him to suit herself.

JOEL McCREA: Catch of the season because he doesn't want to be married. Hates dress clothes; likes to pretend he is young Will Rogers. Careless about his appearance. Extremely independent. Earning good salary under contract. He is tall, ungainly.

CHARLES MORTON: A reckless boy; marry him if you wish to reform a man. Once was chased by lady with a pistol. Good looking, curly-headed, medium blonde, about five feet, ten inches tall.

RAMON NOVARRO: Sings grand opera at home and has pleasant voice. Wants to be a priest. Ramon is a student and likes intelligent women. Are you intelligent? Likes to prepare Spanish dinners and would probably make life miserable for family cook. Dislikes large parties and theater openings. Is very sensitive; Novarro's wife must exercise care in talking to him.

BARRY NORTON: Pretty, rather than handsome. Soft brown eyes, wavy hair and baby skin. Wants to return to native Buenos Aires to live. Is earning nice salary as star in foreign version pictures. Recommended to masculine mannered women.

JACK OAKIE: Likes to appear at formal affairs in white sweater and flannel pants. Smart cracks constantly and doesn't care who; therefore, likely to offend your maiden aunt. Likes automobiles painted with flashy colors. Always late for appointments. Likes to sleep mornings and stay up nights. Attends every prize fight and wrestling match within reasonable traveling distance. Will expect wife to go with him. Steer clear of Jack, ladies, unless you're red blooded.

GEORGE O'BRIEN: Six feet of brawn. Hugs like a bear. Has gypsy nature and wanders away alone and without warning. Dislikes frail girls. Earns huge salary and is very wealthy. Has eluded feminine lures for ten years; hard to get. Wants several children and expects wife to have them. Interested in politics and may follow that profession when screen career ends.

DAVID ROLLINS: Five feet, eight inches tall. Dislikes noisy parties or people and very bashful. Blushes easily and abhors naughty jokes. Ladies, if you are inclined to be broadminded, beware of this one.

HUGH TREVOR: No longer an actor; just a six-foot stock broker with blue eyes and sandy hair. Handles his drinks well and is popular among men. Slices consistently at golf and curses like a sailor's parrot on occasions. Recommended highly for romantic appeal by Betty Compson.

GRANT WITHERS: Doesn't pay the grocery bill (according to ex-wife's divorce complaint) but if you can take care of that little item, this six-foot, two-inch, blue-eyed young semi-brunette is a likely prospect. Hot headed, but soft hearted. Is fond of Grant Withers and wife can get anything she wants by catering to him.

There they are, the bachelors of Hollywood. You takes your choice, or you leaves 'em alone. Pick yourself a man, ladies.

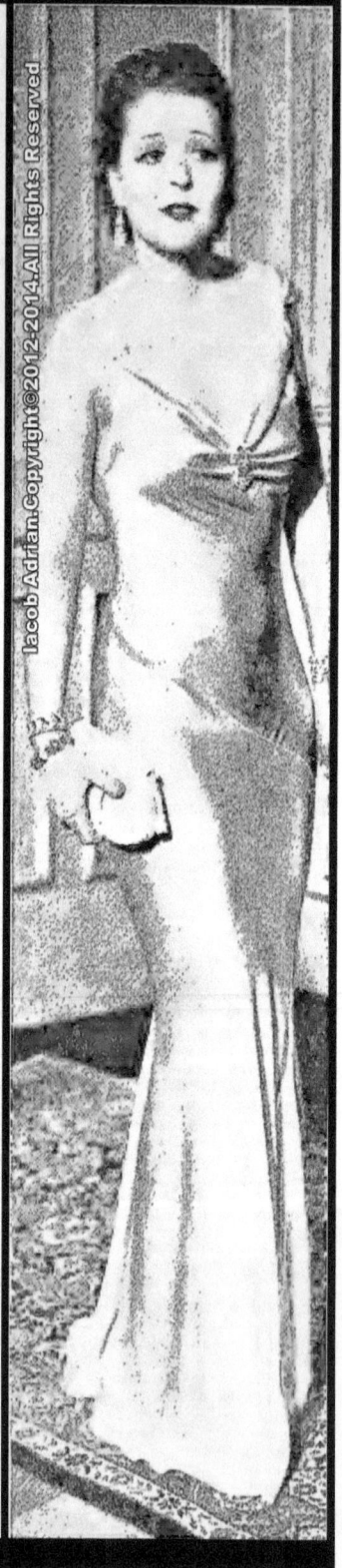

There, Little Girl, Don't Cry

around to print, quote or exaggerate what you say and do!

We were a very small party that night and, when Clara came in, Jack King (with whom I have written many songs) was at the piano. We were singing some of our latest efforts. The Flame of Brooklyn sat in the corner of a large divan, looking very much like a little girl who has been told to behave herself at the party, until Jack played "How Am I To Know?" At that moment he struck a definitely responsive chord on the somewhat strained heart-strings.

Clara walked over and leaned on the piano. Her eyes like two enormous brown pansies were dewy as we sang, "Oh, how am I to know that it is really love that has found its way here!"

She started to hum softly and I never heard a more seductive sound. Having listened to her sing in a rather husky voice in one of her pictures, I was startled by the viola-like quality of her tones.

"Why, my dear," I said, (and sincerely), "you've got a voice!" If my memory is as good as I claim, Clara said, "Nuts!" If it is not, that was probably the first time she ever refrained from saying what she thought. Anyway, inside of ten minutes Jack and I had her singing the scales. Up and up she went, like a plane gaining speed and strength as it acquired altitude.

"Atta girl!" Jack would say as she went a note higher.

"Breath deeply. Push here," I said with my hand on the seven-thousand-dollar-a-week diaphragm. "Bravo!" Eddie Goulding cried, "She must do a musical version of Nell Gwyn!"

WHEN we parted that night I felt that contact was established. Clara knows I am for her, I thought, and suddenly realized that my own diaphragm was sympathetically sore.

One night I came home from work somewhat tired. The phone rang and I was told that Bow was going into the revue and they wanted Something About the Navy! Well, I knew a lot more about the Army. I literally ran to the piano, however, and taking "Columbia, the Gem of the Ocean" as a basis, wrote the song she finally sang, "I'm True to the Navy Now."

A few days later I was told that Clara liked the song and the idea, and asked if, quite unofficially, I would run through the song for her and give her any suggestions that I might have. Would I?—having longed for over a year to direct her, write a song for her, or a story—in fact, do anything to help fan that flame of genius which seemed to be smouldering in resentment!

She came to dinner and between each course, (Am I bragging? There were only four) she said, "Do you really think I can do the song?" After dinner I sang it for her. She sang it for me. I sang it again with suggestions. She listened and, with all the quickness of a cat and none of the other characteristics, accepted and followed the suggestions!

The night that they shot the scene I gave up a party to be there. She was still saying she couldn't do it, but I thought she was swell and so did every stage hand, chorus man, and electrician. That is one reward for being yourself no matter what you are—the people who do the real work in any walk of life admire the person who can afford a high hat and who chooses to go bareheaded!

SEVERAL months passed. Clara made two or three pictures that were considered good. I was still with Mr. de Mille, but I heard from my pals at Paramount that Bow was back, slim, full of pep and "rarin' to go." Every effort was being made to secure a really fine story for her.

There, Little Girl, Don't Cry

Again the ever-changing tide of public opinion rose, surged and snapped at the lurid details published in the newspapers anent Miss Bow and her home life as given out by Miss Devoe, who did not hesitate to try to distract attention from the strength of her own misdemeanors, to the weakness of Clara's mistakes!

Once more the little Bow was broken, but this time she had an arrow, swift, sure and sane. Rex it was who made accusations and answered them with the same cowboy smile. He gave up all thought of his own work. He placed himself between Clara and the mob who had misquoted, misunderstood and misinterpreted her for so long that it was a habit! "Clara Bow!" they murmured. "Hot copy!"

"Clara Bow!" Rex answered—"the girl I happen to love; and if you get near enough to her to put her in wrong it will be over my body, horse, spurs, lariat and sense of justice!"

IT was over them all that I finally, after a month of indecision, got to talk to Clara. Will she resent sympathy, I thought, or does she need it? I then realized that no matter what she wanted or needed, I wanted to be in on what was happening. I picked up the phone. . . .

"Miss Bow is too ill to talk over the phone," said a very pleasing voice.

"Who is this?" I answered.

"Rex Bell!" And there was a challenge in his tone.

"You tell Clara that Elsie Janis wants to talk to her!" I answered the challenge!

Clara's voice was weak, tearful, and her cough racked my ear.

"You and Rex," I said (never having seen the lad), "are coming over here to dinner. I want to see you both!"

There was a long conference, or it may have been a kiss, but they came to dinner. The rest of that evening they remained my guests and I cannot write about it, but I learned that the young man's head is as long as his hips are slim; his mind is fairly one track, but if it had twenty tracks they would lead to Clara! Which is as it should be.

If you are very observing you may have realized that I have a weakness for Clara Bow. I admit it, but my weakness does not let me down far enough to ask anyone to give Clara a break, or a chance to come back or any other sobbing request!

I hope she doesn't come back, though I know she can.

I hope she will grasp the happiness that they gypped her out of when they grabbed her from the peace and security of poverty in Brooklyn and threw her onto a throne made out of executive minds and public opinion, which can be pulled out from under anyone who sits upon it, for any reason, such as holding the sceptre upside down or putting a few extra pounds on the place where even kings and queens sit!

Be sure to begin Clara Bow's own, authentic, signed story, in which she tells the truth never before published, starting in next month's NEW MOVIE MAGAZINE, on sale in Woolworth stores, March 12th.

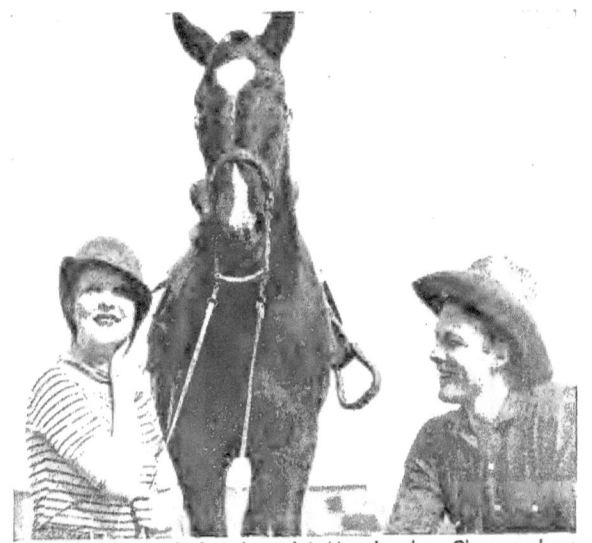

Clara and Rex on the latter's ranch in Nevada, where Clara won her way back to health.

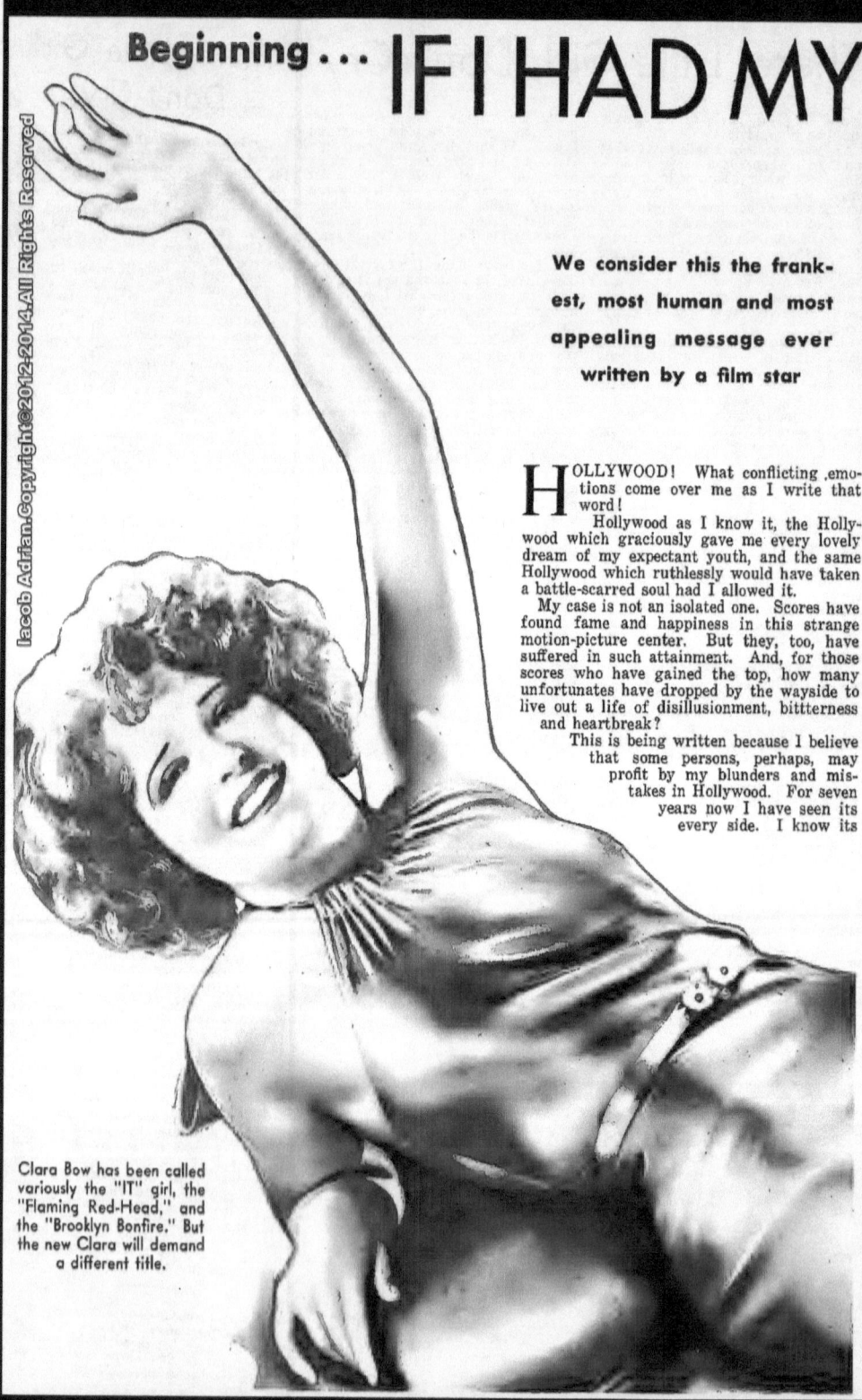

Beginning... IF I HAD MY

We consider this the frankest, most human and most appealing message ever written by a film star

HOLLYWOOD! What conflicting emotions come over me as I write that word!

Hollywood as I know it, the Hollywood which graciously gave me every lovely dream of my expectant youth, and the same Hollywood which ruthlessly would have taken a battle-scarred soul had I allowed it.

My case is not an isolated one. Scores have found fame and happiness in this strange motion-picture center. But they, too, have suffered in such attainment. And, for those scores who have gained the top, how many unfortunates have dropped by the wayside to live out a life of disillusionment, bitterness and heartbreak?

This is being written because I believe that some persons, perhaps, may profit by my blunders and mistakes in Hollywood. For seven years now I have seen its every side. I know its

Clara Bow has been called variously the "IT" girl, the "Flaming Red-Head," and the "Brooklyn Bonfire." But the new Clara will demand a different title.

LIFE TO LIVE OVER

CLARA BOW ... for the first time ... reveals the intimate details of her cyclonic career

beauty and its fascination. I know its selfishness and its venom.

If any individual is qualified to show Hollywood in its true light, I believe I am. That is the reason for this writing. Maybe it will bring some good to others who attempt to follow in my footsteps.

Fortunately I stand in a very enviable position when I make that statement. After many years of intense suffering and bewilderment, I now stand at an intersection on my own highway of life with three distinct roads to happiness directly ahead. The terrors of my past have been forgotten. I am healthy in mind and body, and, above all, I am happy.

If I like I can resume my motion-picture career. I have had many offers from the legitimate stage. In the event that I decide to retire from professional life entirely, I shall return to the ranch where some of the most glorious moments of my life have been spent, and settle down to a quiet existence as Mrs. Rex Bell, and this latter plan appeals to me greatly at the moment.

In the event that I do return to motion pictures, it will be because I appreciate what the public has done for me during my many troubles, and would like to show them the real Clara Bow on the screen before I put Hollywood behind me forever. But more about my personal plans later.

DURING the past year I have been asked this question many times:

"What advice would you endeavor to give a girl who was trying to make good in Hollywood?"

Also: "If you had to do it over again, how would you approach motion pictures?"

In attempting to answer the first question, let us go back and look at the Clara Bow who was just making her screen début. I say this because I think I understand thoroughly just how every young girl feels about Hollywood and a motion-picture career. I know what it is to dream and scheme and imagine oneself a great celebrity in the film world. I know, like tens of thousands of other girls, what it means to cherish that secret ambition to become a star. I know the wishes and prayers and hopes of all of you, hanging on to that slim thread of chance, that perhaps some day in its own mysterious fashion Opportunity will seek you out. How well I know your feelings and thoughts!

WHEN I was ten years old I knew what I wanted. To be a screen star was my idea of heaven. But what chance had I? My family was poor. My mother was in ill health. My father, when he worked, was always a good provider, but he was not always employed. We lived in a not-too-pleasing section of Brooklyn, and my only contact with the screen was an occasional visit to a neighborhood theater, paying my admission with pennies and nickels earned by taking care of neighbors' children when not looking after my mother.

Even in those days, and up until the time I was fourteen, I had but one objective—that of becoming a player in the movies. Sitting there alone in the darkened theater, I studied the movements of my favorites. I did not know good acting from bad, but instinctively something within me revolted at portrayals which, to my mind, were off key. Alone in my bedroom at night I would re-act the portrayal, according to my own interpretation, in front of my mirror. I also was an "expert" in make-up, which always mystified my mother. Appearing in her presence with lips heavily smeared with red and a whitish powder, I never failed to draw the parental wrath.

For days she searched my bedroom for cosmetics but found nothing. The truth of the matter was that the wallpaper in our flat had a decided tinge of red coloring. I discovered that this coloring would come off quite readily, and so with the true touch of an artist I colored my lips with dabs of tint from the paper itself by dampening my finger.

I relate these incidents to show that I, like so many girls of today, was obsessed with the idea of going into motion pictures. How this could be accomplished was quite beyond my comprehension, but just at this time Fate—or luck, call it what you will—presented what seemed to be the golden opportunity.

This was the turning point in my life.

UNBEKNOWN to me, my father had sent a snapshot of me to

the publishers of a movie magazine who, at that time, were conducting a beauty contest. Imagine my surprise when a letter arrived one day stating that I had been declared the winner. According to the rules of the contest, the winner was to be given an evening dress and also a rôle in a motion picture.

I was in seventh heaven. My prayers had been answered. My whole future and happiness had been secured. What luck!

But things were not so easy. Weeks went by. My dress had been delivered to me, but where was the rôle which was to mean the start of my career? I haunted the offices of the publishers until finally they arranged to place me in a production then being filmed in New York.

I shall never forget my first day on the set. I was just one of the mob. No one paid the slightest bit of attention to me. Being told to make up, I watched others apply deft touches of grease-paint and tried to duplicate their procedure. It was a pitiful job, I realize now, but how wonderful I thought I looked at the time. Finally the director, Christy Cabanne, gave me a "bit." It was a crying scene. "Can you act, kid?" he said. I was so frightened I immediately burst into tears. This seemed to please him, and before I knew it I was in front of the cameras. Even to this day I can remember his faint praise of my effort when the scene was completed.

WHAT a thrill! I was now a full-fledged motion-picture actress, and only fourteen years old. I was the idol of the neighborhood. Those children who had heretofore passed me by now were my staunch friends. For hours I had to relate my experiences in the motion-picture studio. This certainly was the ultimate in happiness. But little did I know how fickle Fate can be.

After months of anxious waiting, the picture finally came to our neighborhood theater. It was titled "Beyond the Rainbow" and its star was Billie Dove. Full of anticipation and delight at seeing myself on the screen, I assembled all the children for blocks and borrowed enough money to purchase tickets for those unable to pay their own admission.

The story unfolded on the screen. Reel after reel went by,

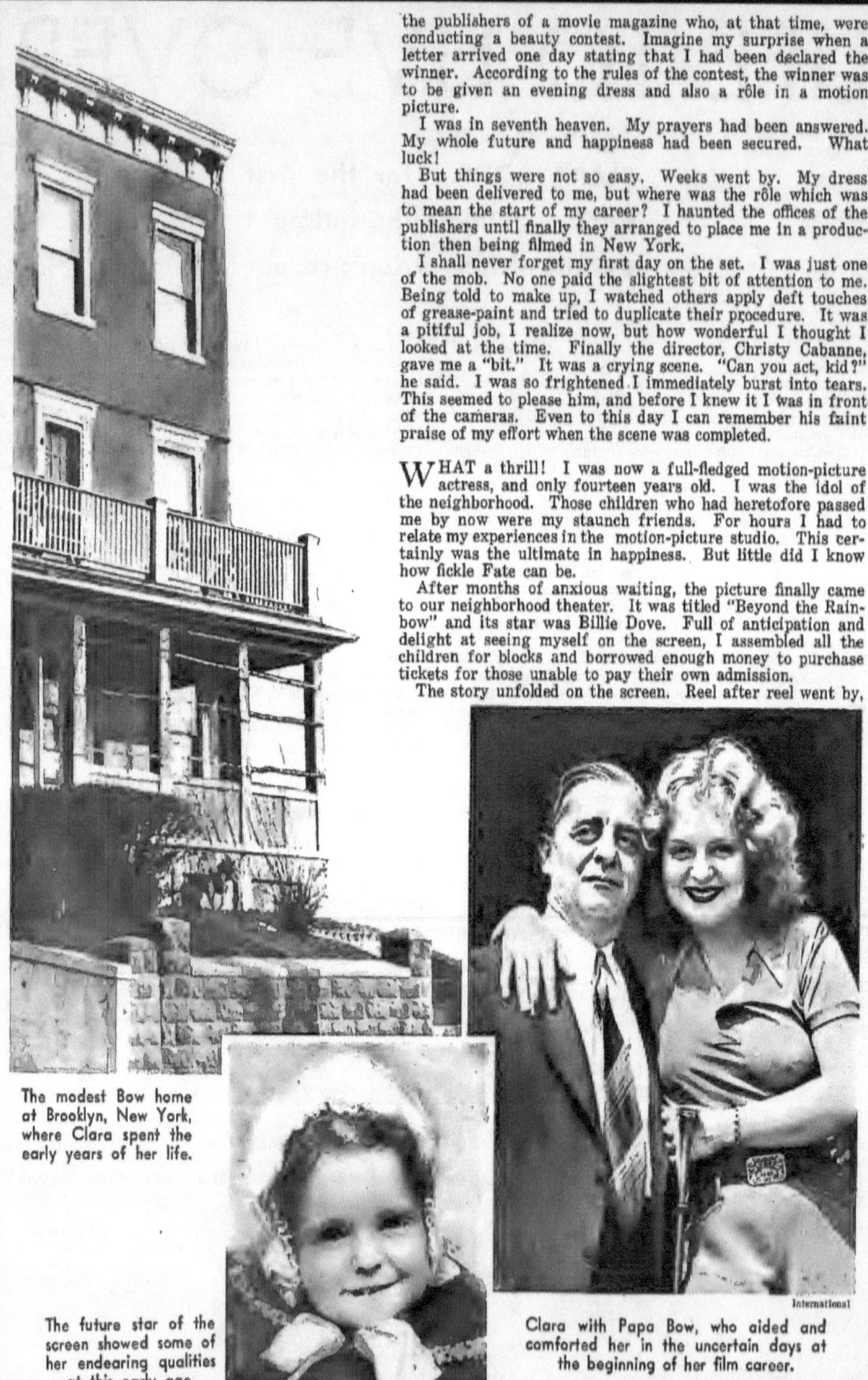

The modest Bow home at Brooklyn, New York, where Clara spent the early years of her life.

The future star of the screen showed some of her endearing qualities at this early age.

International

Clara with Papa Bow, who aided and comforted her in the uncertain days at the beginning of her film career.

but there was not even a glimpse of Clara Bow. My companions became annoying with their taunts, intimating that I was perpetrating a gigantic hoax. Reel after reel went by until the final fadeout, and I had not appeared in one foot of film. I had slumped down in my seat. The tears came and were blinked back. But when the jeers started I could stand it no longer. I bolted from the theater, ran all the way home, locked myself in my room and sobbed as though my heart would break. This was the end. All my hopes and plans went crashing to earth in one smashing blow. To a sensitive girl of fourteen it meant that her whole life was ruined. How could I ever face my friends again? Life just wasn't worth living, that was all.

HOW foolish that seems as I look back at it, but it was everything to me then. My mother, ill as she was, understood, and her thorough gentleness and sympathy eased the hurt. But, despite her understanding and care, something within had snapped.

In an indifferent way I took mother's suggestion to use the money I had earned and enroll in a business training school. She believed that, in this way, I would put thoughts of the screen entirely out of my mind. Reluctantly and sorrowfully I agreed.

Then Fate again entered the scheme of things in crazy fashion.

A month or so after my first motion-picture "flop" I was called one day to the telephone. The man speaking at the other end of the wire introduced himself as Mr. Elmer Clifton, and asked if I could see him that afternoon. My heart took a leap. Elmer Clifton was a motion-picture director, and, hardly daring to believe that good fortune was again in my path, I readily agreed to see him.

So excited I could hardly talk, I spent the balance of the morning preparing myself for the interview. I knew my age was against me. I couldn't play child parts, and yet I was too young for ingénue rôles. So, with one sweep, I tucked away my long curls, put on one of mother's dresses and set out for the appointment, very much a lady of the world.

When Mr. Clifton saw me his jaw sagged. "Why, you're not the girl whose picture I saw!" he exclaimed. "She was just a youngster. No, I'm afraid I can't use you!"

In one brief moment the world crashed around me again. He did have a part! And I had lost it because of my own short-sightedness! Mr. Clifton was leaving.

"Oh, no, Mr. Clifton," I cried. "This isn't the real me. Look!"

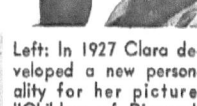

At the right: This is the picture with which Clara won the Beauty Contest in 1922.

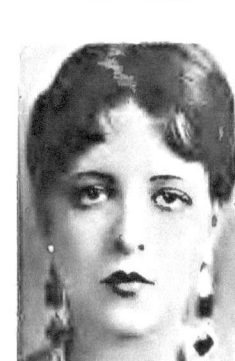

Left: In 1927 Clara developed a new personality for her picture, "Children of Divorce."

At the right: 1928. One of her pictures in this year was "Red Hair."

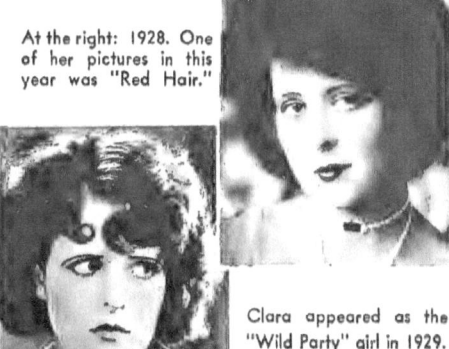

Clara appeared as the "Wild Party" girl in 1929.

Right: At the height of her screen glory. This photo was taken in 1930 while playing in "True to the Navy."

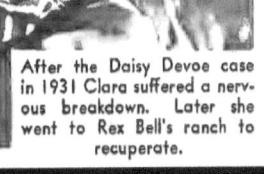

After the Daisy Devoe case in 1931 Clara suffered a nervous breakdown. Later she went to Rex Bell's ranch to recuperate.

CLARA BOW continues
her DRAMATIC STORY

If I Had
MY LIFE TO LIVE OVER

**Through recklessness and impulsiveness Clara
made many mistakes in Hollywood.   And she
gives her viewpoint with absolute frankness
and understanding**

THIS was my first experience on a Pullman. I
knew we were going to sleep on that train but
where I couldn't figure out. I searched everywhere for a bed. My pride held me back in asking such questions of my agent. I thought we were on
the wrong train. Hours went by and still the mystery.
We had dinner. And then, upon my return to my
space, the porter asked if I cared to have my berth
made up.

I nodded dumbly and then watched him go through
those deft motions which are known only to Pullman
porters.

He probably thought I was crazy as I sat and
giggled in open amazement.

I have purposely given the reader an insight into
my childhood to show that, in answering the question: "What advice would you endeavor to give a
girl who was trying to make good in Hollywood?"
I can give my viewpoint with absolute frankness
and understanding.

I, too, had the dream. I, too, was ambitious and
at the same time I was shy and super-sensitive. I

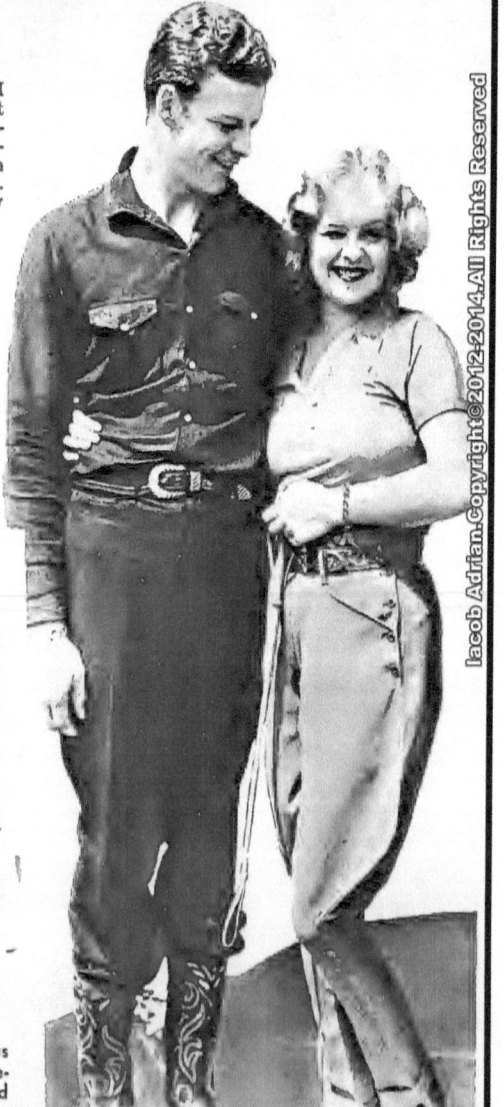

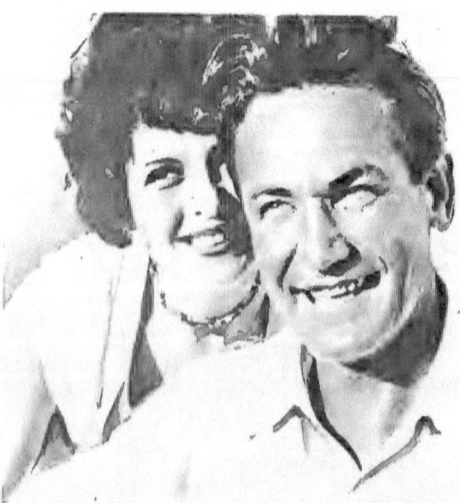

Above: Clara Bow and Victor Fleming. This photo was
taken in 1926 just after Clara had announced her engagement to Director Fleming. At the right: Clara and
husband, Rex Bell.

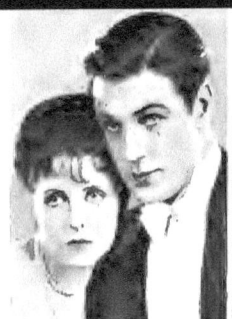
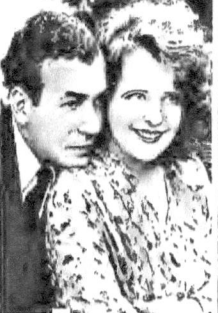
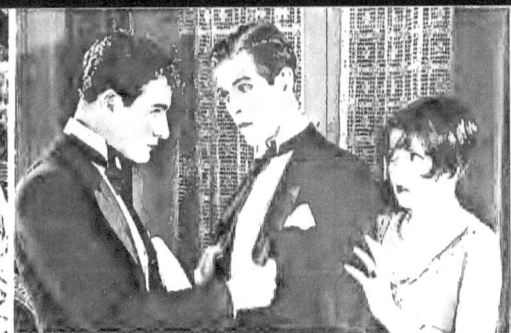

At the left, above, Clara is shown with Gary Cooper, to whom she was reported to be engaged. At the right, with Harry Richman.

At the time this picture was taken, Clara was engaged to Donald Keith, in the center. Later she became engaged to Gilbert Roland, left of the group.

saw Hollywood as Utopia. I see Hollywood-now as it really is. I've tasted fame and wealth and love—true love—and I've also suffered heartbreak and disappointment as much as any individual in the motion picture world. Some scars I shall carry on, my soul forever, despite the fact that I now am in a safe harbor of love. Through recklessness, thoughtlessness and impulsiveness, I had made many mistakes. But I've profited by such errors and that is why I am attempting to assist those who will take the advice of one who knows.

I do this in a spirit of appreciativeness. During my recent troubles, when broken in health and on the verge of despair, my many friends of the vast motion picture audience came to my assistance with countless messages of faith and good cheer. To them, I am profoundly grateful and this writing, in a small measure, is to let them know just how much I appreciate their feeling and thought. And, if I do make another motion picture, it will be to please to the best of my ability those fans and friends who at no time lost faith in me.

NOW then, my advice to a girl trying to make good in Hollywood.

In the first place, don't under any circumstances ever come to Hollywood for motion picture work unless you have a contract, or definite assurance that you will be used in the making of screen plays.

Secondly, don't try pictures if you are unduly sensitive. The work is hard and in the thick of battle many things may be said on the spur of the moment which are not to be taken at face value. It is part of the game, but it will cause heartache unless one's sensitiveness can be overcome.

Thirdly, destroy the illusion from the start. Hollywood is no fairyland. Success comes to those with talent and ability who are willing to face hard work, to make such sacrifices as are demanded.

Take good advice and ignore bad, but be sure you are able to differentiate between the two.

Don't let your feelings run away with your good judgment.

When you realize you are wrong, admit it. When you know you are right, FIGHT!

Be yourself at any cost.

And, above all, don't be what is known in Hollywood as "a good sport"—that is, going against your better judgment for the sake of sparing someone's feelings. It isn't expected in any other line of work and it should not be expected in motion pictures.

But it is!

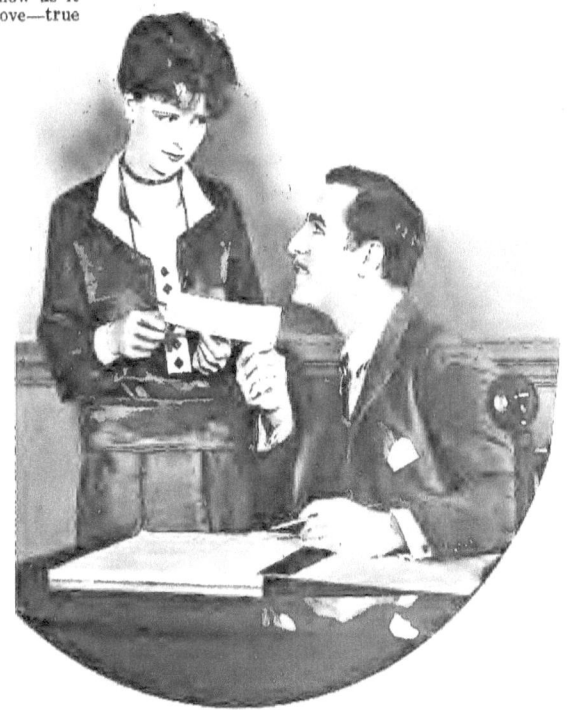

Clara and Antonio Moreno in a scene from the picture "It", which Elinor Glyn wrote especially for Clara.

ALL my illusions about Hollywood were quickly dispelled. Here was no Paradise. Here was a busy little community devoted, for the most part, to the manufacture of motion pictures, a business which ranked near the top among the country's greatest industries. Big business: here were no princes or princesses. Charming men and women, yes; and many who were not so charming.

My trip across the country had not been a happy one. After the first night, the balance of the trip was made in tears. I was homesick, terribly so. My father had been unable to leave Brooklyn and I missed both him and my mother. Settled in a tiny Hollywood apartment with some friends, the agony grew worse. At

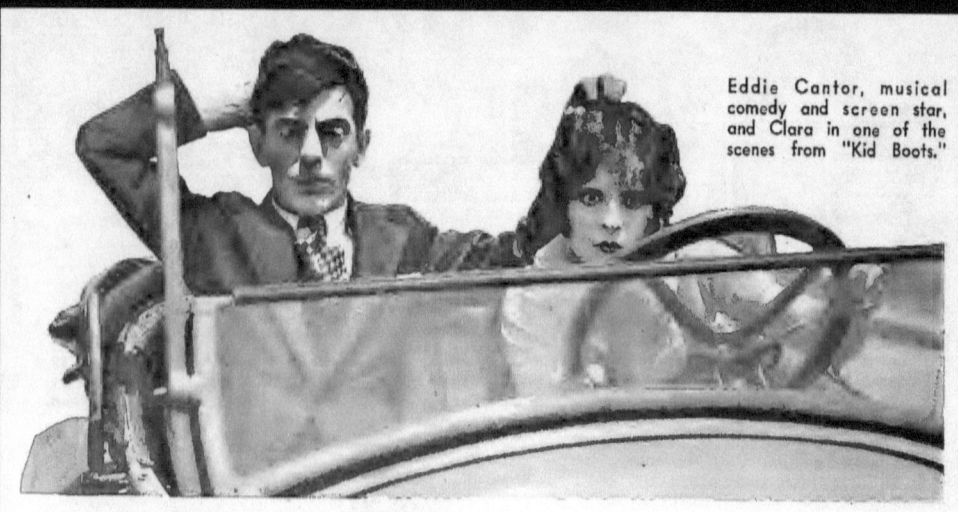

the studio they were considerate but not impressed. Mr. Schulberg was kind but he was also busy with his screen interests. I had nothing to do but think and that became a bore after a while.

Then came news that I was to go to work after all. Mr. Schulberg could not use me in any of his productions at the time but there was nothing to prohibit him from "farming me out" to other producers for small roles. This he did and for many months I seemed to run from one studio to another.

Looking over my records I find that I played in twenty-seven productions in not so many months. But, as time went on, I was getting no place. Always the instructions were the same:

"Clara, X Blank wants you for a 'bit' in their picture which starts Thursday. Run over and find out about wardrobe, will you?"

ALWAYS a "bit." If this was Hollywood I wanted no more of it. This thought I included in my letters to my father, finally threatening to throw over the whole business and return home. Worried at my unhappiness, he heeded my plea, sold his business and arrived in Hollywood to make his home with me. We took a small bungalow in the hills and, under his comforting and advice, the world began to look brighter.

Romance had touched lightly upon me up to this time. Of course, I met many nice boys and went to dances and to the theatre with them just as any other girl would do. But even the intimation of love was far from my thoughts. I had a career to think of.

Gradually, I became better known. Occasionally my name would creep into the billing on pictures and executives of the various studios were nodding now and then when I ran across them on the lot. I was getting somewhere.

It was at this time that I got my first taste of what is known as adverse publicity. What made a tremendous impression on me was the fact that I was entirely innocent— a victim of circumstances.

I had been invited to attend a party at the Ambassador hotel and included in the guests was a young man by the name of Robert Savage. We had a pleasant evening and I saw him several times later. Imagine my consternation when, one morning, I picked up a newspaper and found that Mr. Savage had slashed his wrists after writing some verses which purported to have been directed toward me.

That was my first realization that my name meant something; that Clara Bow was news in the eyes of the public, something which I have realized to a much greater extent during subsequent years, many times to my great humiliation and regret.

That is something every girl who goes into motion pictures must learn. If you do make a success of your work, your name is of public interest and where a girl in non-professional may be allowed certain liberties, a screen player is allowed none without attendant publicity.

I WAS making headway and more money and, as I look back on it now, I believe I must have been quite happy. At this time Mr. Schulberg moved over to what was then Paramount-Famous-Lasky—now Paramount Publix Corporation—

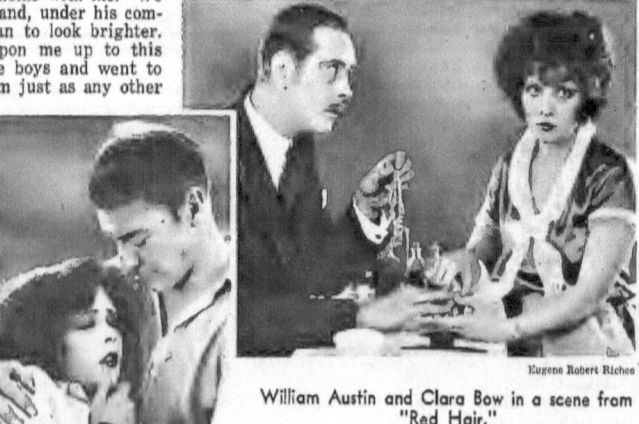

Eugene Robert Richee

William Austin and Clara Bow in a scene from "Red Hair."

Clara appeared with Clive Brook in the picture, "Hula" in 1927.

If I had

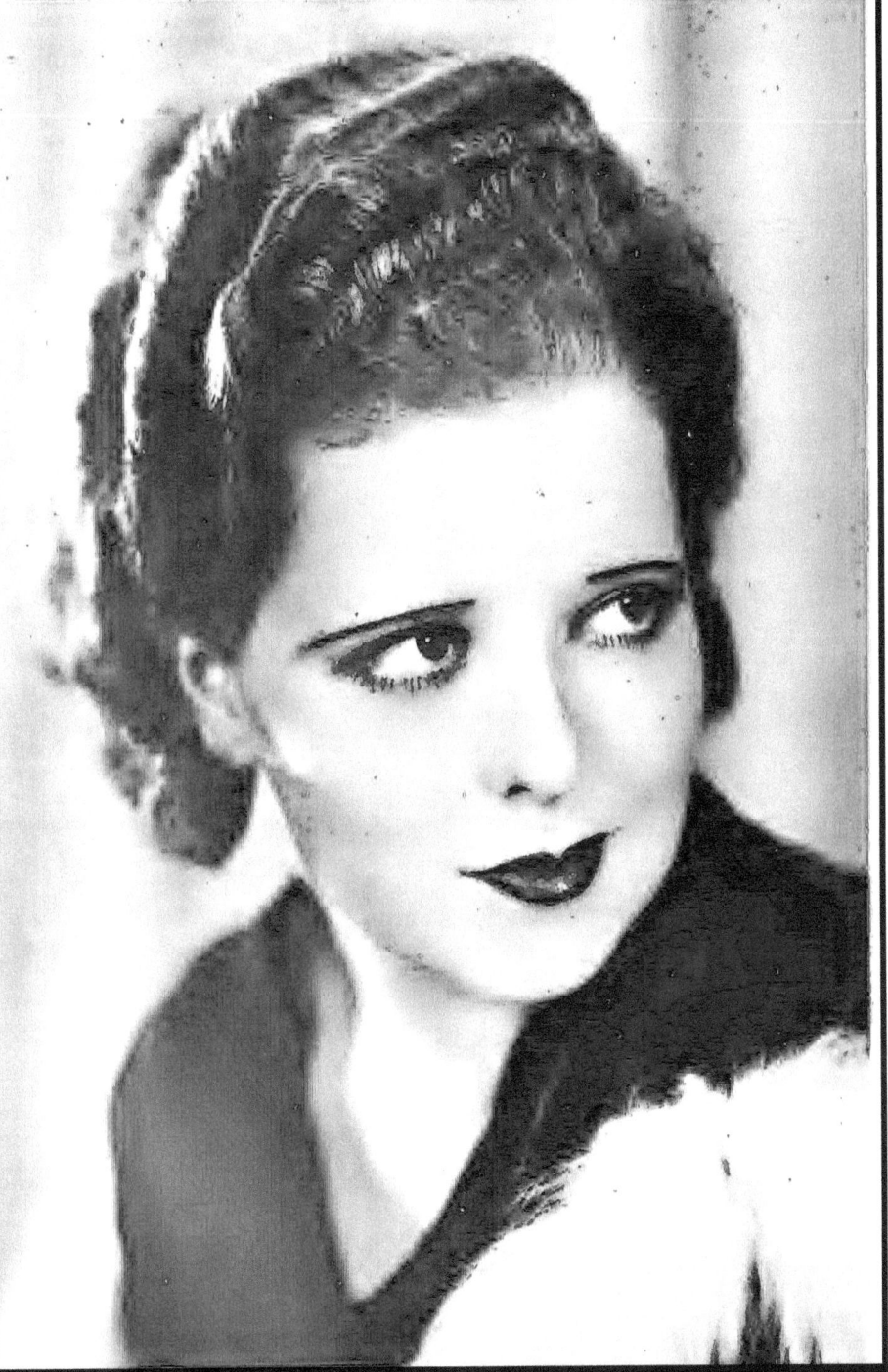

my Life to Live Over

**What is to be the future of this girl who has tasted
the sweetest and the bitterest moments of life?**

BACK in Hollywood I was restless. The picture wasn't going so well. My house was always full of people, some of whom I knew, others I did not. It seemed that my life was not my own. I fretted.

Could this be the fame I had sought so eagerly not so many years ago? Was this sort of life the realization of my dreams? Who were my friends? Daisy, Rex, Harry—you could count them on the fingers of one hand. My name was news, and the slightest ripple on the surface of my existence was a signal for the descent of newspapermen to place my name in headlines.

So this was Hollywood, and fame and fortune! Where were the real things in life? Was I to continue like this?

Don't think for a moment I was ungrateful. I know full well what Hollywood has done for me. I appreciate this to the utmost. But, after all, I paid for everything. If not with money which I earned myself, then with heartaches. I was brittle in the Hollywood sense of the word. I was not able to shake off that sensitiveness of my early childhood. I never shall be able to shake it off. And it ground deeply into my soul when hurt.

With my mental attitude in this condition, came rumblings. If I had only been able to foresee the results! I would have given anything gladly to have avoided such events but, as usual, with my trusting nature, I could not see the danger signals.

Daisy was handling all my accounts. I scarcely gave them a thought. She ordered everything for the house, paid the bills and, as far as I knew, everything appeared to be in ship-shape order. Daisy was changing. It took me a long time to realize this, but after a while it became apparent.

Her friends were the ones who frequented my house. And, at times I wondered whether she was the motion picture star and I her secretary, or vice versa. However, there was no outward rupture. I remained silent principally because I was too weary and ill to argue about anything. But finally things came to a crisis.

Things just couldn't go along as they had been going during those few months. I believed there would be no animosity on Daisy's part, and that we certainly would remain friends. Once again my trusting nature betrayed me. Apparently Daisy had no desire to remain my friend.

Daisy began to talk. I don't believe to this day that she maliciously and deliberately set out to hurt me. But talk travels rapidly in Hollywood, and before it gets very far the original

Clara is happily married to Rex Bell (see photo at right) and is living at the latter's ranch not far from Hollywood.

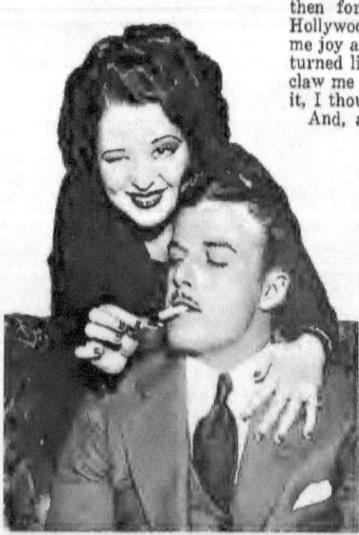

comment has been distorted and twisted to suit the taste of the gossiper. Rumors, ugly rumors, began to spring up about me.

At the same time, an accountant who was looking over my books found strange discrepancies. Daisy, when she left, had several belongings of mine in her possession. These I endeavored to recover.

There were threats which I ignored. Daisy was using the newspapers to tell her side of the story. Knowing publicity as I did, I remained silent, keeping my own counsel, and wishing above all that the entire affair could be forgotten. I held nothing against Daisy. I was the one to blame. So why all the uproar?

But Daisy would not stop and, before I knew it, the matter was in the hands of the District Attorney. This is the first time I have mentioned Daisy De Voe in print, and I would like to say now that at no time did I desire to have my former secretary prosecuted. I felt sorry for Daisy then, and I feel sorry for her now. But the law stepped in and took everything out of my hands. Even a note I sent to the judge in all sincerity failed to sway the verdict of the court. And, Daisy was convicted.

The strain of her trial was telling on me. Never would I have been able to go through with it had it not been for the unswerving loyalty of the man who is now my husband.

However, the trial itself was mild compared with the subsequent ordeal I was forced to undergo.

When I was approached on the matter of paying money to keep statements about me from appearing in print, I was dumbfounded. What in the world could be said about me that already had not been printed? I had done nothing. I knew the statements to be entire fabrications. But what could I do?

There was only one thing I could do and retain my self-respect. That was—fight.

I gave my decision from a sick bed.

This, I thought, is the end. I shall vindicate myself, then forget Hollywood forever. At times, Hollywood had been like a godmother, giving me joy and happiness. At other times it had turned like a vicious old hag, threatening to claw me apart, body and soul. It isn't worth it, I thought.

And, at this time, I learned just exactly who my real friends were. Not the "friends" who follow in the wake of a celebrity just for the sake of their own selfishness, but those who stick by you in the face of adversity.

Do I need to say that the one who aided me most was Rex Bell? The following weeks were torture. Newsboys went through the streets of Los Angeles and Hollywood shouting their messages that in their arms was the "true" version of my inner life. They stormed the various studios with their story which, even though unfounded and grossly malicious, was bound to poison the minds of many readers.

Those were trying days. I dared not expose myself in the

If I Had My Life to Live Over

daytime. I could not sleep at night. Why, I asked myself time and again, does this sort of thing have to happen to me? How can anybody think of such lies and, furthermore, why should they wish to wreck my whole life with such slander?

Sick as I was, I began to take stock of myself. All my years in Hollywood came back to me. All the years of my youth passed in retrospect. I realized that I could have licked Hollywood but, instead, Hollywood was licking me. Who was to blame? I was the one to blame. My impetuosity, my generosity, and my trusting nature all were responsible for my dilemma.

I reasoned, you are not through yet. Get what strength you can and wipe the slate clean before you abandon pictures and the city in which they are made. You have friends, many of them. Your fan mail shows that those who loved you on the screen still love you and have faith in you. It is your duty to vindicate yourself for their sake, if not for your own.

LOVELY Rex. How well he understood. How he stood by me when things looked the darkest. When I made my decision to fight he said: "That's the spirit, honey! We'll fight!"

With him at my side, I did fight. Not because of a spirit of revenge. I wanted to hurt no one. But I did have to clear myself and I did, although it nearly killed me.

After a court verdict had been brought in my favor I was so weary I did not know which way to turn. I thought I was through with motion pictures. I wanted to be. I never wanted to see Hollywood again. I wanted to get away from everything. Discouraged and heart-broken, my future meant nothing. Paramount, to whom I was under contract, realized my feelings and, through mutual agreement, released me from further obligation. Again Rex took control of the situation.

"It's the ranch for you, Clara," he said. "Come on. I'll get mother and we'll all go up there where you can regain your health."

I consented with alacrity.

Just a word more about gossip and rumors. It is true that I was just about as "low" mentally at this time as any human being can be. But the reports which emanated from Hollywood stating I had attempted suicide are grossly magnified. At no time, regardless of the strain I might have been laboring under, have I contemplated such a step. I'd rather fight and now, come what will, I am convinced I can face it with a sane outlook.

Hollywood has been good to me and it has been bad. But, between the two, it has given me "tempering" which has equipped me for whatever lies ahead.

My marriage? Just this. I have realized for a long time that I truly loved Rex Bell. I have been asked how to tell true love from sham. It is a difficult thing to put in writing. All I know is that Rex is loyal, tolerant, understanding, devoted and—of prime importance—he is not jealous. He knows I act on the spur of the moment. He knows that I jump at conclusions. But he makes allowances for my actions,

something I cannot change over night, and he trusts me.

Loyalty, tolerance and trust are wonderful things. Add to that devotion and you will have no trouble in differentiating true love from the sham.

Not so many weeks ago I suddenly had a desire to travel. I decided to go to New York. I telephoned Rex.

"All right, dear," he said. "I'll fix up your transportation. Where do you want to go? New York?"

"I guess so," I said.

That very same night he put me on the train but before doing so he called up Harry Richman.

"Clara leaves tonight, Harry," he said. "Take good care of her while she is there."

In Albuquerque next day I wondered why I was going to New York. I turned right around and went back to Rex.

Our marriage was sudden, yes. For months Rex had asked me to set a date. But I put it off.

On Thanksgiving Day he approached me again.

"I don't want to hurry you, Clara," he said. "But here is the situation. I love you and I know you love me. If you keep putting the marriage off there is a possibility that something might come between us. We don't want that to happen. Marry me now."

So, without saying anything to anyone, we left Hollywood for the ranch—a place I have come to love. Several days later, we were married at Las Vegas, Nevada.

And, for the first time in my life, I am happy. I'm looking at the future through eyes which have been brightened by Hollywood and eyes which have been dimmed with tears countless times because of Hollywood. But, as I say, I believe it has "tempered" me.

I have gone into rather intimate details about my life to show that I have suffered. That suffering, I think, gives me the right to advise and this is what I shall try to do.

TO go back to the question: "What advice would you give a girl who is trying to make good in Hollywood?"

First of all, don't come to Hollywood unless you have a contract to work in motion pictures.

If you have a tremendously sensitive nature, don't attempt pictures, regardless of your ability, unless you feel within yourself that you can avoid the hurts and buffetings which are bound to come.

Wipe from your mind any illusion that Hollywood is a Paradise. It is a pleasant place in which to work but work you must. Nothing is going to be handed you on a silver platter in the motion picture world.

If you are fortunate enough to get a chance on the screen, make up your mind that you will work harder than you ever have worked before. There are hours behind the camera which only the initiated know anything about. Study—hours of it. Consultations, fittings, interviews—oh, countless appointments which are never dreamed of until you are part of the industry.

Pick your friends with great care. They mean a great deal. Don't be "high hat." There is no necessity for it. Be gracious and considerate. It

will pay great dividends. But don't lean over backwards in trying to be nice to those who you know are not sincere. There are plenty of wonderful, steadfast friends you can make in Hollywood. They are charming, intelligent and sincere. Cultivate them. They will round out your life.

And, may I repeat this statement just once more? Don't let your feelings run away with your good judgment. In Hollywood you have to "be on your toes" every moment. Competition is keen. Figure things out before you make decisions and never, never, never act on impulse.

IF you have "temperament," get rid of it before coming to Hollywood. Stand up for your rights but when you are wrong admit it and admit it cheerfully. It will get you a great deal.

And, be yourself. Don't try to imitate celebrities. If you have potentialities, they will be "discovered" although it usually takes time. There is no such thing as being boosted to stardom and fame "overnight," as some of the writers would have you believe. It takes hard work, sacrifice and many times heartache.

I have mentioned being what I call "a good sport" many times in this story. That is, going against your better judgment for the sake of sparing someone's feelings. Please let me say it again. It is one of the lessons you must learn. Take my advice in this one instance. Don't be a "good sport" if it is going to make you suffer.

I wish I could tell you more at this time about my future plans but things are very indefinite now. I am happy. I am married to the man I love. Just playing the role of being his wife is paramount in my mind.

Many offers have come to me asking my return to motion pictures. I feel just this way about it. If a proper story can be found, one which will appeal not only to me but my many friends among the motion picture audiences, I shall probably make at least one more screen play. I do want to please those thousands who have stuck by me through my many troubles. It makes me very happy to realize they were always pulling for me. And, to please them, to show in some small way my gratitude, I would like to make at least one more picture.

In the event that a suitable vehicle is not found for me I probably will say goodbye to Hollywood forever, so I take this means of thanking my many fans from the bottom of my heart.

There is a possibility that I may go on the legitimate stage but this depends, to a large degree, upon the condition of my health. Right now I am in splendid condition, thanks to Rex's loving care and the life on the ranch. But, whether or not I could stand the strain of ten performances a week on the stage is something I cannot tell at this time.

And, remember, I am now a wife.

I hope this little writing will help many with eyes turned toward Hollywood. If you do attempt motion pictures, remember what I have said. And, to all of you the best wishes of Clara Bow.

BACK TO NORMAL

WITH CLARA BOW

Making the movie weight was Clara's first step in her come-back campaign—she showed a loss of 28 pounds in three months and here is how she did it

By ANN BOYD

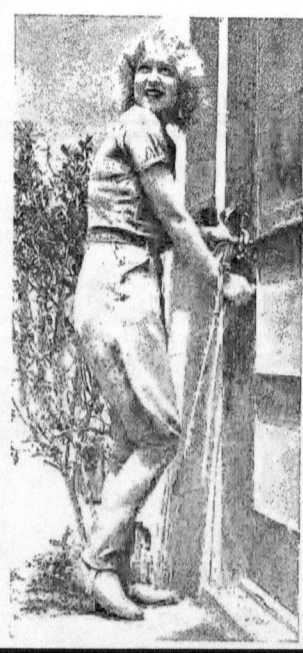

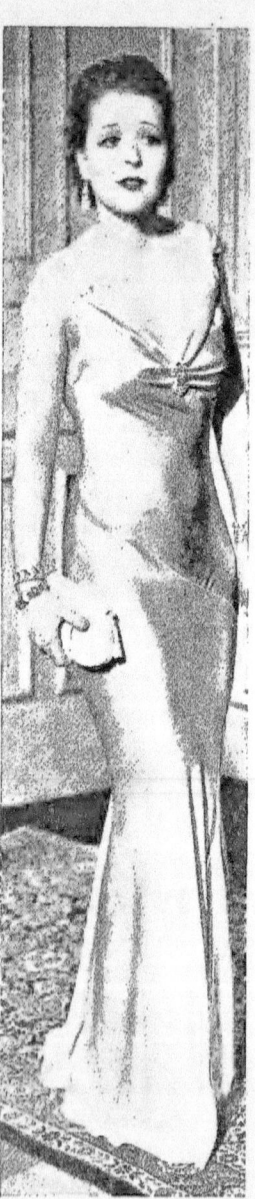

I NEVER took such a beating," said Clara Bow, "but I knew I had to do it and I never missed."

It wasn't merely the daily beating Clara got at the hands of an expert masseuse she was thinking of then but the whole reducing routine that made her come-back to the movies possible. It was the hour of exercise every morning, including breathing so deep as to cause dizziness, the cold showers to keep her skin taut and fresh and the regulated meals.

"But I feel so much better, so much happier," she smiled. "It was certainly worth it. And for anyone who doesn't have to lose a few extra pounds for the camera's sake the routine wouldn't be at all bad.

"I don't think anybody should diet unless they're under supervision. Everybody reacts differently to a diet and anyway figures have taken on more curves than they used to have."

Sylvia started Hollywood on the exercise diet and gave them a chance to cut the strenuous food dieting. She believes in exercise along with a sane and sensible diet—a three-meals-a-day routine—recognizing that sweets are particularly helpful because of their quick energy value.

Here are two of Clara's exercises in her own words:

1. "Stand up tall. Stretch your arms over your head. Breathe in as you rise up on your tip toes and breathe out as you go back on your heels. Breathe as deeply as you can.

2. "Bend over and touch the floor. Swing up and bend back as far as possible.

"Do these over and over again until you are warm and perspiring."

Then Rex Bell, Clara's husband, announced he was hungry so Clara fussed until he had a big bowl of soup in front of him.

"You know," he said, between mouthfuls, "Clara learned to cook out at the ranch, and can she make swell chocolate cake!"

"Oh," said Clara, "he likes any cake, good or bad. He eats two pieces anyway but when he eats three I know it's good."

"But about the reducing," she said, "I'm keeping up the routine and I'm not ever going to get so heavy again. Imagine—145 pounds. I'm 117 now."

Ranch life brought Clara up to 145 pounds—witness the photo at the left—but a course in exercise and massage together with a sensible diet brought her back to her best weight—117 pounds with IT in every ounce.

Bibliographic sources :

Hollywood (1934-1943)
Publisher: Hollywood Magazine, inc. ; Fawcett Publications, inc.

The New Movie Magazine (1929-1935)
Publisher: Tower Magazines, inc.

This documentary study use,
combined in various proportions,
elements from the following categories,
forms and subsets :
- fair use
- documentary
- documentary photography
- feature
- journalism
- arts journalism
- visual journalism
- photojournalism
- celebrity photography
in order to :
- employ material as the object of cultural critique ,
- quote to illustrate an argument or point ,
- use material in historical sequence,
providing independent opinion,
using photos, press articles, advertisements,
opinions of fans etc. ...

www.ingramcontent.com/pod-product-compliance
Lightning Source LLC
Chambersburg PA
CBHW021018180526
45163CB00005B/2005